PT
1/2017
loved it —
very interest·····!

MW01153293

BATTLETOWN WITCH

BATTLETOWN WITCH

Leah Smock,
the Evolution of Witchcraft,
and the
Last Witch Burning in America

Acclaim Press
MORLEY, MISSOURI

Acclaim Press
— Your Next Great Book —

P.O. Box 238
Morley, MO 63767
(573) 472-9800
www.acclaimpress.com

Book Design: Rodney Atchley
Cover Design: M. Frene Melton

ISBN-13: 978-1-942613-46-6 / 1-942613-46-6
Library of Congress Control Number: 2016908455

First Printing 2016
Printed in the United States of America
10 9 8 7 6 5 4 3 2 1

This publication was produced using available information.
The publisher regrets it cannot assume responsibility for errors or omissions.

CONTENTS

INTRODUCTION

This book is divided into two parts, each a book unto itself: the chronology, beginning in Part I, continues sequentially through part II. The book is about witchcraft and, more specifically, about a witchcraft event in the state of Kentucky in 1840. As I began accumulating material, it became apparent to me that in any meaningful discussion about the burning death of a young Meade County woman, it was important that some definition of American witchcraft and how it came to America, as well as how it found its way into Kentucky, needed to be addressed. We tend to think of ourselves monolithically as descendants of Western European culture, but Native American beliefs and West African cultures had their influence on culture and witchcraft in America. The relative isolation of the frontier, especially in and west of the Appalachians, provided a fertile ground for the belief in witchcraft to take root. The first part of the book deals with the development of witchcraft in Europe and how it came to be in the colonies. Part I explores four differing views of witchcraft and its migration to America. Superstitious people using supernatural means may well have pursued the remnants of an eon's old tradition of healing with herbal remedies, forecasting the weather, planting by the signs, and practicing ritualistic sorcery and divination. Just how these practices became societally ingrained and economically viable also are discussed, as well as how Leah Smock was singled out and perhaps misidentified as a witch, invoking the wrath of her neighbors. Anthropologically speaking, a trait is something culturally inherited. Crimes or ethics are defined as taboos or mores. Witchcraft is a trait found in all cultures and considered in all of them an evil influence. The others vary from culture to culture.

Part II of the book deals with the Leah Smock event in its historical context. It tells about the socio-economic environment of the area in which she lived and died and as much as is known about her family, life, death, and afterlife. Contemporary witch trials are discussed geographically and chronologically, while discussing how various Native American and other cultures contributed to this melting pot of occult practices. Part II tells about the sorcery of the time and addresses the tools and traditions associated with witchcraft, as well as discussing various trials and historic cases, including a witch murder in 1928 and a charge of witchcraft in Kentucky in 1929. The book answers a valid question about whether it could happen again. The purposeful burning of Bridget Cleary in Ireland in 1895, the last recorded witch burning, is discussed. Anecdotal stories are told about Leah's apparitional appearances and other afterlife manifestations reported by people who have experienced them. Part II concludes by discussing the anthropological aspects of how and why the expansion of witchcraft occurred. The book concludes at the end of Part II with predictions for the future of technology and its application to the supernatural. To better understand witchcraft, we can look at the resurgence that started with books written and published in the 1920s and 1930s. These books sparked new interests in old practices, and today there are a number of devotees that claim to practice witchcraft as an old religion continuing unchanged from the Neolithic period in Europe. There are some legitimate arguments that can be made for the persistence of a Stone Age religion lasting into modern times, but the preponderance of evidence put forth for this theory is tenuous. It is largely built on the writings of two anthropologists who independently shared the same ideas: Dr. Margaret A. Murray, who wrote *The Witch Cult* in Western Europe in 1921 and *The God of the Witches* in 1931. Dr. Gerald B. Gardner, who studied Malayan culture while serving as a civil servant in that country, wrote four anthropological books. The first of which was entitled *The Kris and other Maylay Weapons*, followed by three books on magic and witchcraft, written after he was introduced to a group of New Forrest witches and initiated into their coven. The first of these books on witchcraft was entitled *High Magick's Aid*, followed by *Witchcraft Today*, and lastly *The Meaning of Witchcraft*. The latter books debuted after World War II. At the end of every war, spiritualism and other occult practices re-emerge, I believe out of a desire by the living to reconnect with relatives, friends, and loved ones killed in the fighting. That factor, and the popular media's exacerbation of the witchcraft craze, intensified the interest largely because of its portrayal of witches trying to cope in modern times with the stress brought on by 20th century society. Movies such as "Bell, Book, and Candle," starring Kim Novak and Jimmy Stewart, "Rosemary's Baby," with Mia Farrow, and the television show "Bewitched" with Elizabeth Montgomery perpetuated the image of witchcraft being alive and well in our time. This idea was further explored by William Peter Blatty's "The Exorcist" and "Legion."

During this initial witchcraft craze, I studied anthropology at the University of Louisville. From 1964 until about 1974, I wrote several articles and papers on the subject and did a study on the effect war had on the rise of spiritualism. I became a member of the Louisville Society for Psychical Research, better known as the L.S.P.R. That society did clinical testing of people to garner evidence of extrasensory perception (E. S. P.), and occasionally investigated paranormal events and other things. Duke University, at that time, had a department dedicated to this study, headed by psychologist Dr. J. B. Rhine. The L.S.P.R. met at the Louisville Free Public Library at 3rd and York Streets. During my several years with the L.S.P.R., I can factually say that only one gripping piece of evidence of clairvoyance was found, and with that one exception, none who professed to have extrasensory talents was evidenced to actually have them.

Anthropology is composed of two principal subdivisions, cultural and physical. Physical anthropology has to do with racial differences, the physical size of people, migrations, genetics, and now forensic anthropology. It is usually the physical anthropologist that identifies skeletal remains. Cultural anthropology studies all aspects of a culture, such as kinship systems, social systems, music, dance, foods, industry, economies, and all other facets of life, including the supernatural. In cultural anthropology, the supernatural is defined as all things unseen but believed. By applying this standard, religion, witchcraft, myths, legends, ghosts, and spiritualism is considered part of the supernatural. My focus of study was prehistoric Eastern United States Native American archaeology. I became an officer in the Louisville Archaeological Society and The Kentucky Archaeological Association, supervising and co-supervising several excavations, archaeological surveys, and salvage projects. To be an archaeologist at that time, one had to have a degree in cultural anthropology. By 1972, I was almost entirely involved in the anthropology department as a student assistant to Dr. Joseph E. Grainger, in the study of Eastern Native American archaeology.

In 1997, I became an 8th grade-Catholic-school teacher at St. John Vianny and Sts. Simon and Jude Schools. I taught math, science, history, and language arts. I moved to the area of Meade County, where I discovered history oozed up from the ground. There were prehistoric sites, Civil War sites, and cemeteries, and the people I met still told the old stories. Here I met Peggy Greenwell and, through her, Shirley Brown, distantly related in a direct line to Leah Smock. Shirley, my wife Fran, and I have become friends. We work together in the historical society, and we share a love of history and genealogy. I restarted my writing career about a year before I retired, completing a book on guerrilla warfare I began in 1993. In 2014, it was released, but after it was submitted and awaiting publication, I began writing this book. Shirley Brown is a Smock family historian who, with her son David, took many of the photographs shown herein. Shirley provided the genealogy, anecdotal history and family papers, and from this information and research I did and papers I wrote fifty years earlier, this book was compiled.

BATTLETOWN WITCH

Leah Smock, the Evolution of Witchcraft, and the Last Witch Burning in America

Part 1

THE ORIGINS OF THE OLD RELIGION AND THE MEANINGS OF WITCHCRAFT

Chapter 1

A Book is Born

In 1964, when my wife Fran and I married at the ripe old ages of seventeen and nineteen, due to limited vacation time, we did not have a honeymoon, but a year later we decided to visit the World's Fair in New York City. At that time, I had decided to major in anthropology, and I had read almost every book the Free Public Library and the University of Louisville library had on archaeology, prehistory, and the supernatural. In early 1964, I happened upon and read a copy of a book entitled *Witchcraft Today*. In October of the same year, an article appeared in *Life Magazine* about the resurgence of witchcraft as an old religion in England, and it featured a woman named Ray Bone. After reading the *Life* article and the book, I had questions. I felt the Vietnam War might have helped spark the obvious expansion of interest. Six months after I wrote Gardner in care of his publisher, I received a letter from a woman named Monique Wilson, explaining that Gardner had died the year before and that she and her husband were running his museum, The Witches Mill, on the Isle of Mann. She forwarded my name to some people in the States, and I received responses from two different sources. One was from a Kentucky man, and another was from an English couple on Long Island, New York. Fran and I met the English couple in the summer of 1965 while visiting the World's Fair. We were absolutely charmed by them (no pun intended), and they agreed to engage in discussion and answer questions I hoped would lead to a future book. Now, fifty years later, I am writing that book. They had a terrific sense of humor, and the husband waxed philosophically about traveling. When I complained about the high cost of airfare, low by today's standards, he agreed with me and said, "There are only two groups of people who can afford to travel: the very, very, rich or the very, very, poor." They had two dynamic children. One of whom was amazed at the way I ate. He said, "Mom, look! He eats one at a time like I do!" I did not understand until they explained that, in England, you don't eat your peas and then your mashed potatoes and when you finish them, go to another food on your plate. You take your fork and kind of mix your food together, and with each forkful, you get a little bit of everything. Upon meeting and interviewing them and some of their friends, someone quipped about our Southern accents, saying we would soon have everyone in New York saying, "Youse all."

The woman was a healer and an herbalist. Her remedies and cures became so well known in the neighborhood that many mothers with children would send them to her when they had a rash or ailment. She also concocted salves and other remedies and had a rather impressive herb garden. She gave Fran some recipes for her herbal remedies. I was suffering from an eye ailment, and she brewed up an eye-wash for me from fennel seed that really helped. They were full of information. We took lots of notes and copied leaf upon leaf of paper.

I must address how paganism or the old religions affected Christianity. The reason this is important is that the old pre-Christian religions have many of the same holy days and similar practices, such as baptism, virgin birth, washed in the blood, atonement, crucifixion or death, and resurrection, to name just a few of the similarities. That these religions borrowed ideas from each other is an undeniable fact. Until about 376 A.D., there were three major religions in the Mediterranean World: Judaism, Christianity, and Mithraism. Christianity and Mithraism were the two most dominant beliefs. Of course, there were other religions, such as the pagan Druids that were not put down by the might of Rome until the 5th century, and there were pagan religions of the Norse and the Germanic tribes, as well as others. Christianity was a rival religion to Mithraism, and one thousand years later, it eventually won out and overtook all rival pagan religions. However, doing so meant that Christianity had to capture some of the allure, thoughts, and ideals that brought people to those religions. Appropriating the pagan holy days and festivals and giving them a Christian impulse was one of the ways employed. Why is this important when discussing witchcraft? It is important because many people believe that, by incorporating these ideas and ideals, Christianity has in a way preserved for the world the last vestiges of paganism. The old religion of the Neolithic cave people may well have evolved into the pagan witch cult of the medieval period until the Church became strong enough to wipe it out through the Inquisition. The pagan religions celebrated similar dates and times of their rites, as did their religious and political rival Christianity. Since all religious holidays are based on the two solstices and equinoxes, people devoted to both religions knew the moon, sun, and star signs and the seasonal changes to the earth. These seasonal changes affected the breeding seasons of animals, planting, and harvesting, as well as cultural traits, such as clothing and shelter, and they still do. The people were tuned in and learned of herbal remedies and the zodiac. They used observations of nature to predict the weather, direct the people when to plant, and perform rituals to make it rain or cease raining. Some of these same things are still being practiced by herbalists, faith healers, and the rural folk in the Appalachian Mountains, as well as the hills and hollows of old Kentucky, North Carolina, Tennessee, Virginia, Pennsylvania, Georgia, and Alabama. These people today are not pagan in the sense of being unenlightened, unsophisticated, or non-Christian. They are generally God-fearing Christians who go to church regularly yet keep the old lore alive and in use. In Amish communities today, the use of herbs is well known. Whether this is because of economy or something more, Dr. Gary V. James wrote, referencing the Amish, "They are usually pretty intelligent, and they seek medical care when they need it. But they are very frugal and will basically try anything to keep from coming to see a doctor. They do a lot of folk stuff—herbal remedies and stuff like that, but I enjoy taking care of them."[1]

There are two factors that seemed to promote and influence the use of herbal remedies and folk cures before the 20th century; firstly, there was a lack of trained doctors and that was especially true during the 17th and 18th centuries; secondly, there was virtually no money with which to pay for their services. Even if the payment of money could be made, there simply were few doctors on the frontier. Those that existed were located in or near towns and cities. This meant that every person, when sick or injured, would accept help from any person nearby willing to provide treatment. Over time, these country healers were looked to as important members of the community. Midwives who delivered babies were usually healers and herbalists. During the Civil War, this was especially true since most of the doctors young enough to enlist were called into the war service. The doctors left at home were often too old to work or perhaps retired. They did what healing they could, but the midwives and their male faith healer counterparts were kept busy.

Even as late as the early 1900s, the breadth of medical knowledge was sorely lacking in Appalachia. My grandfather, Arthur Clarence Bryant, graduated in 1912 from Western Kentucky Teacher's Normal School in Bowling Green, Kentucky. That school is now Western Kentucky University. His degree allowed him to teach school and qualified him to be an accountant. The entire length of his course of studies was six months. He proudly told me, "Son, if I had gone another six months, I could have been a doctor." The reason he didn't go the additional time was because he didn't want to spend the following year after he graduated as an intern for another doctor. One hundred years ago in Kentucky, one year of schooling and one year of internship was all there was to being a doctor. Taking that information into consideration, a folk healer and herbalist with a few successful years of experience was probably as qualified, if not more so, than a medical school graduate with his total two years of training. In general, people on the farm took care of each other and went to the doctor when there was no other choice. An example of this is pointed out in a story about Arthur Clarence Bryant. I have heard two accounts about how his hand was injured and either account could have caused the injury. One story was that he was opening a jar of preserves that my grandmother had canned and the jar broke, cutting the palm of his left hand severely. The other story fits with what Papa was doing on the farm. During the Great Depression, he would buy unbroken mustang horses brought into Bowling Green from out west. He would pay $2.00 a head for them and take them back to his farm, heal them if they were sick, and break the horses, so they could be ridden. Even considering that a few died when broke to the halter and able to be ridden, he sold them for $12.00 a head, a considerable profit during the Depression. The other story states that while he was on the ground, one of the horses stepped on his hand, bursting it open. Either way it happened, he wrapped a handkerchief around the hand to stem the blood and to keep out dirt. It was late in the evening and getting dark. Mamaw Bryant lit a coal oil lamp and set it on the kitchen table. Papa washed his hand, poured coal oil into the wound to disinfect it, sat down with a needle and thread, and sewed the palm of his hand together. There was no anesthetic and only the flickering orange glow of the lamp. The hand healed with only one minor problem. The injury cut across the heart-line of his palm. Whether because of the poor light or because he was in a hurry to get done, he did not get the lines in his palm connected properly, so the heart line ended and picked up again about ¼ inch away. I always wondered what a palmist would think should one ever try to read that palm. That story is not unusual; rather, it was typical of doing what one had to do in the absence of a doctor.

In Western European countries, each shire or community had a wise person or two who did the healing, told the peasants when to plant, read the weather, and gave advice. Occasionally, they would make good luck charms and advise on how to protect against bad luck or evil spirits. These Western European traditions carried over to the American Colonies and were as necessary here as they were there and evolved over time to become folk healer/faith healers existing in the Appalachians today. In Pennsylvania and eastern Ohio, hex signs can be seen on barns. These are amulets designed to protect the barns and livestock. Other signs can be found in Appalachia.

When I came to settle in Meade County, Kentucky, I became fascinated with the stories and the people of the county. There is a tremendously rich heritage of history and family relationships that are captivating. As I met and talked with many people who I am glad to say became my friends, little-known or forgotten stories were told me. I have written numerous articles in weekly newspapers and in historical and nostalgia magazines recounting these tales. One of the most interesting stories had to do with a woman, a girl really not much more than twenty-two years of age, who was burned as a witch near Battletown, Kentucky. I decided this story should be told, not only because of the time and the environment in which it occurred but also in an effort to explain this tragedy. The girl, Leah Smock, is probably the only person in America to be burned for being a witch. All of the other known executions were by hanging, with the exception of one man being crushed by stones. Burning, like beheading, just didn't catch on in the States. In this book, I deal with the subject of witchcraft, magic, charms and spells, herbal cures, faith healing, religion, and the modern resurgence of occult practices, but this story is really about the lynching of a beautiful young woman because of the fear that she was a witch. It tells of the effect it had on the people in her community and her family in old Lapland, now Battletown, Kentucky. The strange events that occurred before her death convinced the community of her guilt and malicious intentions. Mysterious things that have happened since her death continue to affect the people of the area to this very day.

Beverly Furnival, a writer and poet, was so taken with the story she wrote the "Ballad of Leah Smock," herein printed with her permission. Beverly became the secretary of the Meade County Historical and Archaeological Preservation Society (MCHAPS) and currently serves as its president. As a wife, mother, army veteran, historian, writer, and world traveler, she brought a fresh perspective on history and archaeology. She also brought her father, Dr. Warner Sizemore, a learned man and artist, who possesses in-depth knowledge of many subjects, including comparative religion, homeopathy, and herbal lore. Another member, Shirley Brown, a great-great niece of Leah Smock, has given a number of presentations about her great-great aunt to the Meade County Public Library, as well as to MCHAPS. Shirley is an artist, photographer, lecturer, and writer in her own right. Many of her photographs are seen on television. I wanted to write about this period of Meade County from more than the historical event alone; therefore, I drew upon the research I had done as a student of anthropology from 1965 and 1975 when I wrote several articles and papers and presented archaeological reports at various Kentucky universities, as well as archaeological societies.

The English couple we met stated there were no hereditary witches, although witchcraft could run for several generations in a family. Lucy Maier, however, in her scholarly book *Witchcraft*, states that the belief in hereditary witches is common in certain African groups and that the inheritance can be passed along in diverse ways.[2] Hereditary witches, according to Mair, teach the lore to their children, but the knowledge could not be taught to children born without the capacity for it. There are a good many people who believe that there are hereditary witches, and Margaret and Leah Smock, as well as Marie Laveau, may be examples of them.

The stories of Leah Smock, John Blymire, Nelson D. Rehmeyer, the Bell Witch, Marie Leveau, Mrs. Reynolds, Bridget Cleary, and the Craft girls, as well as the Native Americans featured in this book, do not prove the existence of witchcraft, but they do prove these people were believed to be able to control forces beyond the capability of ordinary men and women. The perception of this validated the existence of supernatural forces and that was enough for many to believe. Once their reputation as witches was substantiated, they became endangered by the very perception they had so carefully cultivated. Whether guilty or innocent, they reaped a bitter harvest produced by the seeds they had sown.

Many years ago, I interviewed a faith healer, now dead, who told me the ailment and the cure of the patient are often locked together within the patient's mind. People can make themselves ill with psychosomatic ailments and create symptoms with their minds that generate physical pain brought about by outside influences or fears causing stress. When the patient is treated by a faith healer who captures the confidence of the former, his or her faith in the healer gets them better. The cure may not, by itself, be effective and might not be rendered yet, but it can still be effective because of the confidence the patient has in the healer. The healer with whom I spoke was supposed to help a man with a particular ailment. He told the man that he would prepare the necessary material the next day, and by that evening, the patient would no longer need his services. For one reason or another, this healer was prevented from making the necessary preparations. He felt bad about it, but it could not be helped. Both the healer himself and the patient held steadfast belief that the process involving a Bible reading would heal the patient. The morning after the reading was to be performed, not knowing it had not been, the patient showed up at the healer's door. The healer realized the patient was likely to be angry, so when he opened the door, he immediately told the man he was sorry that he could not do the healing as he had planned. The patient had a confused and then a shaken look on his face. He had been cured, he thought. All of his symptoms went away, there was no longer pain, and he felt great up until the moment the healer apologized. You see, his faith was so great in the healer that, by his belief, he cured himself. Shaken that the reading had not been done and convinced he had not really been healed, he became depressed; although the healer took the necessary measures straight away, they did not work. He had lost his confidence not only in the healer but also in himself, though he was unaware of that fact. His ailment returned, only worse, and the healer could not help. He later told me that he would never make that mistake again. If he had remained silent and let the patient thank him, he would have gone in his own mind from a zero to a hero. It is funny how things work out. Perception can be everything, and in this business, whether faith healing or witchcraft, that is definite.

Chapter 2
WHAT IS WITCHCRAFT?

According to Gerald B. Gardner in his book *The Meaning of Witch-craft*, there are three possible meanings of witchcraft: firstly, there are those that take the rationalist view that witchcraft is a kind of mass hysteria, arising from psychological causes, and there is no such thing. Secondly, there are those who maintain that witchcraft is real and that it is the worship and service of Satan, in whom its devotees appear to be great believers. This is the attitude taken by the prolific writer Montague Summers and his many imitators. Thirdly, there is that school headed by anthropologists like Dr. Margaret A. Murray, who have tried to look at the subject without superstitious terrors and theological argument on the one hand or materialistic incredulity on the other. This school of thought maintains that witchcraft is simply the remains of the old pagan religion of Western Europe, dating back to the Stone Age, and that the reason for the Church's persecution of it was that it was a dangerous rival.[3] Murray makes a strong argument for her hypothesis, but the span of 30,000 years seems too great to expect religious rites to remain largely unchanged. Nevertheless, vestiges of this old religion in the form of dance, chants, and the costumed portrayal of animals in rituals—as well as the more practical type of magic, i.e. the use of plants for healing, the foretelling of the weather, making charms for protection, and practicing rituals to ensure abundant harvest—seem to have survived until the late Middle Ages. Where I have a difference with Murray is in the proposition of the universality of this old religion. Since people 500,000 to 100,000 years B.P. (before present), were making migrations, presumably from Africa, in small bands or family groups of hunters and gatherers, the nature of religious ideas was probably slow to develop because of the effort required for acquiring food, clothing, and shelter. It was during the Neanderthal period that the first ceremonial evidence of religious thought as we know it today manifested itself.

The age of Neanderthal began with his immediate ancestors of 250,000 years B.P. These early Homo sapiens and Neanderthal ancestor are known as pre-Neanderthal. The pre-Neanderthals, *Homo erectus*, were hunting and gathering people living in small bands. Neanderthals are the first cousins of modern man, and his ancestors are known only by the flint tools they left behind. Substantial numbers of these stone tools have turned up, and it is possible to re-create with some assurance the lives these ancient people led.[4] They evolved into the heavier-boned Neanderthal, who exhibited some primitive facial features but whose brain, although shaped somewhat differently, was as large as modern man.

Donald Johanson wrote,

> I consider Neanderthal conspecific with *sapiens*, with myself. One hears talk about putting him in a business suit and turning him loose in the subway. It is true; one could do it and he would never be noticed. He was just a little heavier-boned and more primitive in a few facial features. But he was a man. His brain was as big as a modern man's but shaped in a slightly different way. Could he make change at the subway booth and recognize a token? He certainly could. He could do many things more complicated than that. He was doing them over much of Europe, Africa, and Asia as long as 60,000 to 100,000 years ago.[5]

It is from this group of *Homo sapiens*, "Thinking People," we get our first glimpse of religious thought.

One of the ways archaeologists can notice the effect of religion is by the treatment of the dead. When the dead are subjected to a ceremonial treatment, it indicates a belief in an afterlife. The concept of an afterlife opens the way to the belief in a supreme being or beings, a code of behavior, morals necessary to attain the afterlife, and perhaps the realization of a group of people that can direct the activities of the band toward a more righteous life on earth, ensuring a happy life after death. Neanderthals were the first people found to treat the dead in a ceremonial manner. They may have gotten the idea from some of the animals they hunted. Death is considered by many to be life's bitterest fact, the inescapable defeat at the end of a long struggle to survive and prosper, and man is the only creature saddened by it. Many animals seem momentarily distraught when death claims one of their number; elephants, for instance, have been observed trying to revive a dying member of the herd, even attempting to get it back on its feet by lifting it with their tusks. But only man anticipates the event far in advance, acknowledging it will inevitably occur, dreading it, refusing to accept it as conclusive, and taking some solace in an afterlife. One mark of this behavior is burial of the dead.[6]

It is believed that the earliest humans simply left their dead where they fell and walked away. Some may have placed the bodies in trees to protect them from scavengers, where the body would decay and the bones would later fall to the ground and be dispersed by scavenging animals. This seemed not to be the case of Neanderthal. The first Neanderthal man excavated was likely buried where he was found. Other burials were found in 1885 and evidence shows that fires had been lit over the bodies. Constabe states that the fires might have been to counteract the chill of death, but they could also have provided a vehicle, smoke to carry the soul to heaven. In 1908, the first Neanderthal graves exhibiting funeral rituals were excavated. A body of a man was discovered in a shallow trench, with a bison leg on his chest, and the trench was filled with broken animal bones and flint tools. Although it was not recognized at the time, the animal bones probably were food offerings to sustain the person in the afterlife, while the tools were for his use. An excavated 1960 burial in northern Iraq produced evidence of pollen in a 60,000 year old burial. The archaeologist, Ralph Solecki, had the samples of soil from the grave sent to a laboratory, where the pollen was identified and found in great numbers and even clusters. It is believed that this hunter was laid to rest on a woven bedding of pine boughs and flowers; more blossoms may well have been strewn over the body. Microscopic examination of the pollen indicated that it came from numerous species of bright-colored flowers, related to the grape hyacinth, bachelor's buttons, hollyhock, and groundsel. Some of these plants are used in poultices and herbal remedies by contemporary peoples in Iraq. Perhaps Neanderthals, too, felt that the blossoms possessed medicinal properties and added them to the grave in an effort to restore health to the fallen hunter in the afterlife. On the other hand, the flowers may have been put there in the same spirit that moves modern people to place them on graves and gravesites.[7]

Neanderthal populations began to wane about 35,000 to 30,000 years B.P., at the same time Cro-Magnon man began to expand their range and population. These truly modern men coexisted with the Neanderthal, possibly inter-marrying with them, in an overlapping period of 5,000 to 6,000 years, until about 30,000 years B.P. There is little doubt that some contact between these two cultures occurred. Whether this caused strife between them or conversely resulted in harmony may never be known. But it is safe to think that whatever knowledge could be gleaned, each from the other, served them both well. The funerary practices, music, dance, magic, and healing arts of the dying Neanderthal likely became part of the new culture. Some people believe that Neanderthal became extinct while others believe they simply evolved or became modern man. Whatever they gained from the Neanderthal, Cro-Magnons were already accomplished artists who created engravings, statuary, and magnificent cave paintings.[8]

The Cro-Magnon period was noted by more finely-made flint tools and the fantastic artwork that adorned the walls of the caves they inhabited. They made statues of clay, ivory, and carved bone. Many of these artistic examples are thought to be evidences of sympathetic magic designed to ensure or increase the killing of game. They undoubtedly created works of art on wood, hide, and with feathers, which were not preserved over time. Murray's hypothesis is discussed more completely in the next chapter, but in general she believed that traditions from about 30,000 years B.P. continued more or less uninterrupted until about the 14th century.

Chapter 3

WITCHCRAFT: THE EVOLUTION OF A FERTILITY CULT TO 1400 A.D.

A bout 30,000 years ago in a small cave in southern France, a ritual was held deep within the bowels of the Earth. This ritual was carried out by the men and boys on the way to becoming men who lived in an age known as the Magdalenian. The ritual was conducted in a high-vaulted room, which was found only after a long and trying journey through the passages in the cave of Les Trois-Freres. The walls of the ceremonial chamber were adorned with pictures that rival those of artists of today. Paintings of bison, wild horses, and reindeer, with arrows and boomerangs whizzing around them, appeared. Two sculptured reliefs of bison stood out from the wall, representing a bull mounting a cow.[9] Clearly, Magdalenian man was involved with the ritual practice of magic. These people knew the secrets of copulation, and from the many footprints still in the wet clay floor, they danced and worked themselves up to a feverish pitch, possibly to impregnate the females of the band so that the band would in turn be stronger.

Not only was their magic directed toward fertility but also toward success in the hunt. Many of the animals painted were depicted with arrows piercing their vital parts. It would appear then that, in this period of transition from the late Stone Age to the early Neolithic period, man had become accustomed to worshipping in an organized manner. He was not only interested in the fertility of the band but also of the animals the band depended upon. He apparently drew a picture of the animals he was about to hunt, and then he carefully followed this by drawing arrows and spears piercing the hearts and vitals of these animals. This display of the use of sympathetic magic is little different from the practice of medieval witches piercing dolls with pins. It does not begin with medieval witchcraft but rather with the ceremonies of prehistoric man.

The art of Ice Age man was preoccupied with women and animals. These were the things most often drawn, modeled, or carved by the early inhabitants of the caves. It would seem then that the possibility of a polytheistic religion is likely. At the very least, there was probably a god and goddess representing the duality of man and nature. And it may have included a whole train of animal deities. In the dragon's hole, overlooking the village of Vattis in the Engadine, stood rectangular stone chests carefully covered with flat slabs. Each chest contained a number of cave bear skulls. Large bones of the limbs had been thrust through the eyes and mouth. There was clear evidence man had beheaded the animals and treated the heads in a ceremonial manner.[10]

After the retreat of the glaciers, man emerged from his subterranean home and began the migrations and dispersal of peoples to the plains, coasts, and bogs where new cultures developed. The old vaulted chambers with their myriad of paintings were all but forgotten in the minds of men. All that remained was the half-remembered notion that deep within the Earth dragons, demons, ghosts, and spirits lay a-waiting.

Archaeological evidence is scarce in the areas of Western Europe, so we find ourselves with less late prehistoric information. Generally, we know that man learned to domesticate animals, including reindeer. He learned the secret of plowing and planting the soil, as well as the changing of the seasons with the equinoxes and solstices. He also learned to cast and forge metal tools and weapons. It seems important that in Europe the Neolithic farming cultures existed until the transition into the Copper or Bronze Age. To illustrate this, there are some examples of polished stone axes and flint daggers that are exact duplications of metal originals, including the casting marks. By 2700 B.P., ax and adz-using peasants occupied most of Europe. There is no doubt, however, that hunting, fishing, and gathering cultures, some of which adopted a few of the farmers' cultural innovations, persisted for a long time in many regions that were not particularly favorable for cultivation. And, in some cases, vast regions, such as Northern Europe, remained exclusively the domain of the heirs to the Mesolithic ways of life until the first millennium B.C.[11]

There is little known of what ceremonial and religious organizations persisted or followed after the rise of the Neolithic period and its transition to the Bronze Age. But there is nothing known that would cause a drastic change in the religion and practices of those cultures, only the slow and gradual changes produced by the passing of time. It is my conclusion that many of the religious practices changed very little through the Neolithic period and into the Bronze Age and perhaps even into the Iron Age of Europe. None of the economies of this time were advanced beyond simple farming, and magic and religion of one kind or another are undoubtedly present among all communities on such primitive economic levels.[12] About 120 years ago, Edward B. Taylor pointed out that all peoples in primitive economies believed in animism, that is the existence of intangible, non-material, or spiritual beings, which may be souls, ghosts, ancestors spirits, fauna, flora, ogres, monsters, or simply objects. A more advanced form of religious practice that is found in economies not quite so primitive, such as an agrarian one, is polytheism, the worship of one or more spiritual being. Taylor held that polytheism was a descendent of animism or a step in an evolutionary chain of religious thought.[13] We do have evidence of an archaeological nature to describe some of the features of the Iron Age way of life. This evidence seems to exist in much the same way from 2500 years ago until about 2 A.D. The reason for so little change is likely due to the relative isolation in which Western Europe was swathed.

Iron Age man is still a mystery to us, but thanks to the chemical nature of the peat bogs that dot most of Europe, we have some solid information on his religious practices. Since I am primarily interested in the religious and ceremonial practices of these people, I will not go into detail about lifestyle, architecture, or other matters. Suffice it to say, in general these people were farmers, herders, and gatherers; most were of a peasant class; and on the whole, they were to be considered prosperous.

Their religious practices were a direct throwback to the Neolithic practices aforementioned. They worshiped a god and goddess. They were probably animistic and definitely polytheistic. Their religion concerned itself with fertility. Sacrifices were made to the gods in several ways. Sometimes an offering was made to the gods in the manner of leaving precious articles at the holy places, which were the traditional abode of these gods. Perhaps the most striking, impressive, but abhorrent type of sacrifice practiced by Iron Age man was that of human sacrifice.

It is from the remains of both types of sacrificial offering that we get our only glimpse of the religious ideals of these people. The sacrificial sites at Foerlef Nymlle, Broddenbjerg, and Spangholm illustrate for us the simple shrines of the peasants.[14] This was little more than a stump of a tree about nine inches in diameter and about four feet high, which represented the god of fertility. Around this god figure, bottles, and pottery jugs were placed, probably containing some of the harvest, in honor of the god. In the words of archaeologist Peter Vilhelm Glob, "these sites illustrate for us the shrines of the Jutland peasants, of the Iron Age, where their offerings were made, and where a female and male deity were worshipped in the community. And so it is throughout the land in all peasant communities, small and great; for what could be more important than fertility in field and stall."

The ceremonies surrounding the sacrifice of humans are unknown. Apparently, the victims or volunteers did not expect their death. The bodies that have been preserved in the bogs all have considerable food contents in their stomachs, indicating they were well fed before their death. The method of execution was usually strangulation; in some cases, death was caused by drowning, while blows to the head killed other victims. Only one case has come to light showing a method of execution that caused a considerable spilling of blood—one victim died of a massive cut to the throat.

Methods of interment not only of the sacrifices but also of the peasants themselves show that mortuary goods were commonly buried along with the dead. The bodies were sometimes in a flexed position but more commonly were outstretched. It has been suggested that a flexed burial indicated a return to the womb, referring, of course, to the fetal position of young in their mother's womb. It has also been postulated that a flexed burial might simply be an expedient burial method when there was less time for the interment, calling for a smaller grave to be dug, or a burial occurring in a colder part of the year when the ground was frozen and the digging was harder.

Little is known of the chiefly structure or priestly class. The design of a bracelet used by neo-pagan participants, although made of rose brass, was identified as a copy of an Iron Age high priest's bracelet from Denmark. There must have been some organized system of priests and priestesses in this culture; however, nature worshippers do not normally have elaborate churches or temples. We have to assume that the major rites were held out-of-doors. It is interesting to note that, although there are no definite shrines or temples dedicated to the gods, small amulets in the shape of the fertility goddess are found in abundance in excavations of certain Iron Age village sites. These are charms that might compare to the wearing of a cross or rosary today, but they are doubly important due to the fact that these items bear a striking resemblance to the Neolithic fertility goddess of the Magdalenian period.

The Iron Age people probably had a religion that evolved into a form we now call Druidic. Practically nothing is known of the Druids with certainty, yet many authorities have inferred an elaborate religious and political organization. Some were soothsayers, magicians, and bards. Their religion, known only in fragments, was a cult of numerous gods and natural objects, such as trees, wells, etc., in which magical practices were involved. Assemblies were held in consecrated spots, such as the groves of oaks. Mistletoe growing on the oaks was venerated and used in medicine and magic. It seems likely to me that it could have been used in fertility rites, as well. That proposition could explain why we continue to kiss under the mistletoe even until today. Stonehenge, the circle of upright stones in Southern England that pre-date the Druids, may have been used by them. The Druids wielded great power and all who refused to obey were banished or slain for sacrilege. Roman law and Christianity put an end to the organization by the fifth century.[15]

At the time that Britain was occupied by Rome, the religion popular with the Roman soldiers was Mithraism. It is logical to assume that where soldiers were sent, chaplains would also be present. It seems likely that these priests of the soldiers would act as missionaries to the local people. Considering that the Romans were occupying a land that was the home of the politically-powerful Druids, it would follow that some sort of intercourse was necessary to keep the peace. This could well have been in the realm of intermarriage with the local inhabitants, meaning that the existing cult at least in Celtic Britain was probably modified by Roman and Greek ideas. There are indications of a mixture of Roman and Greek conventions with the existing Druidic religion of the time, best exhibited by the use of runes and their apparent origin.

As early as the second century, the Goths learned to recognize Greek culture and designed a series of signs derived from Greek and Latin cursive script. These signs we now call runes. Following the examples of the Greeks, the Goths gave to each sign a sonorous name. The shape of their letters conformed to their mode of writing and the uses to which they put it. Most of their inscriptions were either scratched or carved. Runes are, therefore, almost entirely rectilinear in form. In the fourth century, knowledge of runes spread to Germany and other Teutonic countries.[16]

It seems to me that the Romans bringing their customs and religious practices to the European peasants, coupled with the Greek influence on runes and quite possibly some of the more popular religious ideas of that time, there was a period of changing religious doctrine. It is important to note that, by the second century, there was little change in the religious ideas from the Neolithic period some 25,000 years previously. After the introduction of Christianity into the world of the Old Religion, for a while the two seemed to co-exist peacefully, but since they were rival religions, the old and the new soon came to blows.

If the term "witchcraft" is synonymous with and used to replace the term Old Religion, which Murray feels is justified, it has had occult and magical overtones since the days of the Druids and earlier. In early Christian days, magicians were believed to get their power from demons or evil spirits—not yet the Devil, who was later thought of as a master and consort of witches.[17] The church would later, as it became more ingrained in the culture, use the concept of the Devil to a greater degree. By the seventh century A.D., however, the influence of one-half century of Christianity had not been sufficient to wipe out the counter influence of the Old Religion, or as Murray prefers, "witchcraft." Theodore, seventh archbishop of Canterbury, in his *Liber Poenitentialis*, the earliest collection of ecclesiastical disciplinary laws, devotes a whole section to magical practices and ceremonies. One of the items mentioned that was punishable was the dressing in the head and the hide of a bull or stag and going about in the month of January.[18] This certainly is reminiscent, if not exactly, of the reenactment of one of the paintings in the Cavern Les Trois-Freres. In that ancient cave, men were depicted wearing the head, antlers, and hide of stags. It would seem, then, that some of the Old Religion's traditions were still alive at this time.

By the year 690, the idea that the Old Horned God depicted in the caves and on Iron Age carvings was when the concept of a horned devil seems to have originated. In England, devil worship continued to be a source of concern to lawmakers and church fathers alike. In 960, Witheraed, King of Kent, issued a code of laws, one of which ordained that if a man made an offering to devils, he had to be fined six shillings or flogged; while the Venerable Bede, in his great work *Historia Ecclesiastica Gentis Anglorum*, refers to devil worship being practiced by another king who appears not to be assured of the efficacy of Christianity. According to Bede, Redwald, King of East Saxons, had an altar to sacrifice to Christ and another small one to offer victims to the Devil in the same temple.[19] Although at this late date it's unlikely, this fact suggests the possibility of human sacrifice. In any event, it seems clear by evidence that both religions were coexisting.

Due to the Old Religion being one of the nature religions, the fact that it had to do with the fertility of crops and animals and the practice of herbal lore and sympathetic magic, it had an appeal to the rural folk. Today not only in Europe but also in our country, rural folk perpetuate superstition. The Pennsylvania Dutch protect their barns and houses with traditional hex signs. Horseshoes are still nailed above doors with their ends up to hold the luck, and the left hind foot of a rabbit is still occasionally found in men's pockets. This appeal is slow to die. It may be because of the inherent need of men to control the uncontrollable, or it might be simply a carryback to the days when we danced in caves. But for whatever reason, it has carried on. The Bishop of Inverkeithing was known to lead the fertility dance in the churchyard as late as 1282.[20]

Christianity had a stronger organization than the Old Religion, and we mustn't forget that the might of the Druids was put down by the force of Rome. Eventually, the Old Religion was forced by fines and other penalties to go underground. But being forced to worship secretly has not in the past proven to be a strong deterrent to worshipping at all. I refer, of course, to the Christians of Rome. The church recognized this, and so in 601, A.D. Pope Gregory wrote to Melitus, his missionary in England, telling him not to stop such ancient and pagan festivities but to adapt them to the rites of the church, only changing the reason for them from heathen to Christian. In this way, the church took over the pagan festivals or holy days and converted them to Christian holy days.

Some of the major pagan festivals we are quite familiar with, while others we know only as Christian holy days. Christmas, of course, is considered a Christian holiday. In fact, December 25 is the birthday of Mithra, the god of the Roman soldiers, and it is an even older Celtic holiday that welcomed the sun at the Winter Solstice.[21] Out of ancestor worship came the use of a ghost go-between, and this became the basis for the Celtic All Hallows Eve. At this time, the last day in October, the Celtic people celebrated the end of the old year and made ready for the new. They danced in queer (meaning odd) masks and queer dress and conceived more than a new year alone.[22] The Christian holiday of Easter, originally called Passover, fell on a spring date close to the Anglo-Saxon festival of the Vernal Equinox. Amongst the Anglo-Saxons, the month of April was dedicated to Eostre (or Ostara), the goddess of spring. It is from her that the holy day of Easter gets its name. Some of the lesser-known festivals would include the Assumption of Mary, celebrated on August 13, which was the Roman festival of Diana. Lammas, celebrated August 1, is the Anglo-Saxon festival Hlafmaesse, The Bread Ceremony, a pagan thanksgiving for the ripening of the grain.[23] The merging of these pagan holidays with Christian doctrines gave Christianity its foothold on the peasant class in Europe. Once that foothold was firmly established, it was from this point that the church began to denounce the old gods as devils, and in later days, it made the time right for more violent persecutions. Indeed, the doors were closing on the Old Religion.

Generally, there were eight pagan festivals, four greater and four lesser ones, as well as a monthly festival of the full moon. I will list below in bold type the Pagan Festival and in Italics the corresponding Catholic celebration. Where possible, I will denote the reason for the celebration in parenthesis:

Pagan Festival
Catholic Holy Day of Obligation

All Hallows Eve, Halloween, October 31: the date Old New Year ended. It honors the souls of friends and relatives now departed.
All Saints Day: a celebration of all Catholic Saints, named and unnamed.
It dates from the late 4th century.

Yule Rite, December 22: the date for celebrating the Winter Solstice, the marking of the time each day becomes longer toward the advent of Spring.

Christmas, December 25: a celebration of the birthday of Jesus, although many scholars think Jesus was born in the spring. The original birthday was set on January 6, the pagan feast Dionysos and Osirus.

Candlemas, the Feast of the Torches, February 1or 2nd: Lupercalia or the old feast of Pan, it denotes the rebirth of the Sun.
Ash Wednesday, February 13: the Holy Day commemorates the beginning of Lent. It did note the Purification of the Virgin Mary and Churching of Women.

Vernal Equinox, or Spring Rite, March 21: This festival celebrates the equal day and night and the fertility of crops and animals. It denotes the planting season. *Palm Sunday, March 24*: the Holy Day commemorates Jesus's entry into Jerusalem.

Beltane, May Eve or April 30: In Germany, this festival is called WalpurgisNacht. This is a fertility festival noted by the erection of the May Pole, a decidedly phallic symbol, which the women danced around, holding ropes or colored ribbons. Riding brooms and leaping high in the to make the crops grow higher is part of the rite. *Divine Mercy Sunday, April 7* (formerly celebrated April 30, *2000*): the day on which the Vatican declared Maria Faustina Kowalski to be St. Faustina. Originally, this was said to be St. Walburga's Day, a Sussex-born woman who immigrated to Germany and died in 780 A. D. (Note: Walburga is an old Teutonic name for Earth Mother.)

Summer Solstice, June 22: the beginning of Summer. This celebration marks the longest day of the year and the shortening of daylight leading to the Autumnal Equinox and the harvest.

The Festival of Saint John the Baptist, June 24. **Lammas, August 1, or July Eve:** This is the Gaelic FireFestival of Lugnasadh, The Feast of Bread, and the Eve Of Lady Day. This is a festival to ensure a good harvest. *Assumption, August 15:* the asumption of the Blessed Virgin Mary upon her death, her body rose into heaven without decaying.

The Autumnal Equinox, September 21: this date marks the equal length of day and night. It celebrates the ending of the year with the

Harvest Home Festival. *The Mid-August date for the Assumption* may serve for both Lammas and the Autumnal Equinox, occurring midway between them. There are also twenty Feast Days in September, the 19 being Saint Januarius's, and September 23 commemorating Saint Pietrelcina.

*Notes movable Feast Days

The preceding listing shows how many of the pagan festivals have likely been adopted by early Christian priests; however, I am not positive that is the case. Most religions have holy days or festivals on or about these same dates, due to the seasonal changes of the Earth. It should also be noted that are numerous Catholic movable feast days not listed on the chart, some of which correspond, and that the Catholic Holy Days are not always the same for preceding and future years. Still, eight pagan festivals show a direct correlation with Christian holidays.

I have taught for about eleven years in a Catholic School, although I was raised in Jones Memorial Methodist Church, attending services as a child with many other families and their children, including Marsha Williams Norman, the 1983 Pulitzer prize winning author of 'Night Mother. Jones Memorial no longer exists but was a very conservative and, I now think, fundamentalist church. Norman's internet biography states she was the daughter of a "strict fundamentalist" Methodist mother. While I did not realize that the church I was in was ultra conservative (because as a child I went where my parents took me), that experience became the norm. Later, my childhood church joined together with several other Methodist churches to become a new combined Methodist Church, and my mother continued attending as a member until no longer able. While I remember Marsha only slightly, being two years older, quite a difference when you are a child, I remember her father Billy quite well, and I think I got at least part of my love of hunting from him.

I have participated and attended many different churches, both Catholic and Protestant, and I believe that there are many different ways to reach a rich reward in the afterlife. I had a near death experience in 2011 where I suffered cardiac arrest, my heart stopped beating, and my breathing ceased for several minutes. While I lay on an operating gurney in this condition, I witnessed a light coming toward me from a hallway, and I have never felt so good in all my life. The closer I came to the light, or the closer it came to me, the better I felt, until I reached a point where I thought I could not possibly feel any better. I was wrong—it got better. I could see two shrouded figures coming toward me in a waist-high flow of golden fluid or fog. They were robed in purple garb, one a head taller than the other. And then, all at once as if a giant vacuum cleaner was turned on, the vision was whisked from my view, sucked away, and I found myself awake and in great discomfort with someone crunching down on my chest. I was awake and back in my body. To this day, I am not sure that "Code Blue" team did me a favor. But here I sit, comfortable that there is an afterlife, and that it is good, if I don't foul it up.

One might wonder why I point out the fact that Christianity modeled itself along pagan lines in order to overcome pagan religious practices and spread itself over a majority of the world. I think that is the way things must be. I have visited and participated in many denominations of Christian religions, as well as some others, including Native American. It is interesting that in the words of Arthur Weigall, noted author and Egyptologist, the last vestiges of paganism now lie within the Christian Church. I believe that is so. To exemplify this, there is a hymn that I first heard in Nativity Catholic Church in Brandon, Florida. Later, I have found it in churches across the United States, west to east, from Arizona to Kentucky, and north to south from Kentucky to Florida. It is called the "Canticle of the Sun", the lyrics by Marty Haugen:

The Canticle of the Sun

Refrain
The heavens are telling the glory of God,
And all creation is shouting for joy!
Come, dance in the forest, come play in the field,
And sing, sing to the glory of the Lord!

Verse One
Praise for the sun, the bringer of day, he carries the light of the Lord in his rays; the moon and the stars who light up the way unto your throne!

Verse Two
Praise for the wind that blows through the trees, the seas' mighty storms, the gentlest breeze; they blow where they will they blow where they please to please the Lord.

Verse Three
Praise for the rain that waters our fields, and blesses our crops so all the earth yields; from death
   unto life her mystery revealed springs forth in joy!

Verse Four
Praise for the fire that gives us his light, the warmth of the sun to brighten our night; he dances with joy, his spirit so bright, he sings of you![24]

This song captures succinctly the spirit of Christianity while preserving the very nature of earlier traditions. It references air, earth, fire, water, sun, and moon.

There was little of importance concerning itself with the practice of witchcraft (the Old Religion) until the early 12th century. It was in the year 1180 that the first mention of nocturnal meetings strongly suggestive of the witches' Sabbath occurred.[25] In 1324, a very important witch trial came up. The trial, which was in Ireland, brought charges against twelve people, some of whom held high standing, the chief person being Alice Kyteller of Kilkenny. They were charged with absenting themselves from Mass for long periods, sacrificing animals to the devil, offering the limbs of these animals at crossroads to a spirit who instructed them to call him the son of Arte, practicing divination, casting spells, and various other charges. Dame Alice was found guilty, but after offering penance for her sins, she was reprieved.[26] It seems that the proposition at this time was that if a person was a witch, then, from time to time, they could be expected to do a little witchcraft.

The idea that Alice Kyteler and her cohorts sacrificed animals and made offerings at crossroads seems to parallel a belief held by the Old Religion. Ancient Teutonic people often built their altars at crossroads, still a common place for shrines, but their religion involved human sacrifices, and this always raised the minor question as to who should be sacrificed. Enterprisingly, they chose their victims mainly among condemned criminals, and the sacrifice did double service as an execution. The sacrificial altar endured at the crossroads in the form of a gallows for some time to come.[27]

By the year 1406, the first real attempt to put down the practice of sorcery, or what remained of the Old Religion, was enacted. Henry IV wrote to the Bishop of Lincoln, commanding him to imprison any wizard he found and institute a strong inquisition against all sorcerers.[28] From this time forward, a combination of church will and civil law did what it could to wipe out all traces of witchcraft or the Old Religion.

It is interesting that the Inquisitions and force used against what might have been man's oldest religious tradition was done in the name of God. Certainly, in their time, the old gods served their people as well as the new one would in his.

The basis for Murray's view of witchcraft being the surviving remnants of the Old Religion is certainly possible when the evidence indicates that a tradition of animism and polytheism has existed in much the same state for 30,000 years, but this obviously broad statement could also be open to criticism. This reasoning is, of course, only one possibility for defining what witchcraft is. We will examine the other possibilities and look upon a new theory I will put forth.

Chapter 4

WITCHCRAFT, A PRODUCT
OF MASS HYSTERIA

I t is general common sense that there is no such thing as witchcraft, and that the Inquisition in Europe and the subsequent witch trials in Salem, Massachusetts, were largely examples of mass hysteria. Perhaps that's true. Certainly, the collective fears of a group of people can lead them to do terrible things. Vigilante justice and lynch mobs come to mind when considering the form that mass hysteria can take. When the civil law and the church doctrine comingle to condemn people for whatever reason, it is fertile ground for hysteria to develop. The French Revolution, the Inquisition, and the Salem witch trials come to mind as examples of that fertile environment. Much has been written about all three of the aforementioned, but I think the Salem witch hysteria and subsequent trials are significant because they occurred in a restricted geographic range and were promulgated by the rules of law brought from England and administered to the colonists. Personalities, politics, false witnesses, spite, jealousy, greed, and bored, frightened, adolescent girls combined to cause the death of twenty-four persons and terrify the population. For this reason, Salem is a prime example of mass witchcraft hysteria without a basis in fact.

The Salem witch craze involved rival families, the Putnams and the Porters, both of whom were important members of the community. Salem Village, isolated from the seacoast and the coastal towns, had an agrarian economy. The Putnams were farmers, while the Porters farmed but also had commercial ventures along the coast and in the Caribbean. Because of their various businesses, the Porters gained wealth and stature in the community, while the Putnams' wealth was static. The trials that began in 1692 were influenced by difficulties between the two families. There were two towns predominately involved with the witch hysteria, Salem Village and Salem Town located a few miles apart.

John Putnam Sr. and John Porter Sr. were the patriarchs of their respective families. Both were influential and liked. Trouble between the two families began over a dam and sawmill owned by the Porters. When the dam was built, it flooded the farm of the Putnams, resulting in a lawsuit brought against the Porters. Later, the Porters took an adverse position to the Putnams when they tried to secure the independence of Salem Village. The Reverend Samuel Parris came to the Village in 1689, and twenty-six of the villagers voted to provide him with a house and barn, as well as two acres of land. Some of the villagers objected to this extravagant gift to the preacher, and in 1691, the supporters of Parris and Porter were ousted from the village council and replaced by members loyal to the Putnams or those who harbored grudges against the Porters. The new committee voted down a proposed tax to pay Parris a salary.

Coincidentally, the witchcraft accusations began in the Parris household in 1692. Parris had a slave girl named Tituba, who was teaching Parris's nine year old daughter, Elizabeth; her cousin, Abigail Williams; and a friend, Anne Putnam, to read fortunes. As the four sat around the table trying to divine the future, Parris returned home from a church meeting and caught them. Probably to slither out of a very uncomfortable predicament, the girls soon began to show signs of being possessed or tormented by demons. They exhibited convulsions, fits, bodily contortions, and purportedly lost their ability to see, hear, or speak. All of this was perhaps an act to fool the adults and gain sympathy, not to mention avoid punishment. When they seemed to regain their senses, they complained of being tortured, bitten, kicked, pinched, and hit by spirits or demons.

Soon the girls began to call out the names of their tormentors, from a child of four to an eighty-year-old man, Giles Cory. These girls seemed to select people to blame for their afflictions from people in and around the village who, for one reason or another, did not fit the profile of a good villager. People like anile Sarah Good, who, though harmless, did not attend church regularly and wandered about the village talking out loud to no one and begging for food. Sarah Osborne was called out, and she had previously caused a scandal by having premarital sex. The girls likely had heard their parents and others gossiping about who was lacking in social graces or who was doing what to whom. These then became the targets of their accusations. In all two hundred people were accused of being witches in the summer of 1692. Of the two hundred accused, nineteen were hanged while one was pressed to death by stones. There were five men and fifteen women executed. Four more died of maltreatment in prison. John Proctor publicly challenged the girls as fakers, and his wife was promptly accused by the girls. The Putnam family was involved with the prosecution of nearly fifty of those called out, and the Proctor family, who tried to calm the village and stop the craze from continuing, found about twenty of their allies charged with witchcraft. Accounts differ on the number of people charged.

This was a reign of terror. No one had to die—those that admitted their guilt and repented could live, but banishment caused their farms and valuables to be put at risk and sold to cover the expenses of their trial and imprisonment, which meant that they would not leave their families an inheritance equal to whatever they had amassed in the estate. At least twenty of them chose death, and some possibly did so as a means to preserve at least part of their estate. This may have incentivized residents who held a grudge or had a boundary dispute to accuse his neighbor. As the victims of witchcraft, the accusers might be in a position to make an offer on the land, after the village government deducted the costs associated with the expense of the trial, imprisonment, and sentence of those tried. The trials lasted four months, beginning in June of 1692, and the last executions were held in September. By October, the hysteria was virtually ended, and by April of 1693, it was completely over.

While there is absolutely no real evidence that there were any actual witchcraft practices, Tituba from Barbados probably carried some occult customs with her from West Africa, where she presumably originated. West African native practices were brought to the New World by the slave trade. There were accusations of dolls or puppets being used by some and nocturnal meetings. It is interesting that the law used to convict these witches was a 1604 law of James I that prohibited conjuration, witchcraft, and dealing with wicked and evil spirits. We know that the victims were falsely accused. Many years later, one of the girls made a public apology in the village. Although likely there was no witchcraft, the hysteria was real and deadly. This does not answer the question: "Is witchcraft real or only hysteria?" The answer is immaterial because it does not need to be real for witchcraft hysteria to bring about the deaths of innocent people. All that is necessary is the fear that witches are real. And that they are capable of harming others.

Chapter 5

WITCHCRAFT, THE WORSHIP
OF THE DEVIL

The last hypothesis given by Gardner deals with the proposition that witchcraft is real, and it is the worship of an anthropomorphic devil. This is the classic medieval church view of witchcraft, likely arising in the middle to late 13th century. In 1486 *The Malleus Maleficarum,* (also known as *Hexenhammer,* or *Hammer of the Witches*) was first printed. It is perhaps the most important and terrible work on demonology ever written. It is a textbook of procedure for the suppression of an underground movement that opposed the Christian structure of medieval society. The leader of this movement was the Devil, and his servants were witches.[29]

Before we look more closely at what witches who served the Devil were supposed to do at their Sabbaths, let's take a look at the Devil, hell, and their origin. Biblically-speaking, Raymond Buckland states that the modern concept of the Devil is a strictly Christian invention.[30] Before the New Testament, there is no mention of him. You will remember that the malevolent animal in Genesis was a serpent equipped with legs or feet of some kind. After tempting Eve, he was doomed by God to crawl on his belly, eat dust, and be under the heel of man. While Genesis does not call the serpent the Devil, that is the implication. He was an evil or malicious tempter. So, we must ask the question, how did a serpent in the Garden of Eden become a horned devil with a pitchfork and an army of demons? In prehistoric and olden times, horns were a symbol of power. If a powerful man was depicted in a statue, sometimes he was shown with horns. Michelangelo even sculpted Moses with horns, giving him an aura of power. Horns in nature are found on some of the most powerful male animals, such as the bull, ram, goat, deer, elk, moose, roebuck, and stag. Horns were a noticeable distinction found among the mightiest animals in the herds. The male of the species used their horns or antlers to dominate other males and amass a harem of females for themselves. In this way, the propagation of the species is fulfilled. The average whitetail buck deer will have a harem of about seven does. Each doe will produce twin offspring, consisting of a male and female. This one-to-one ratio demands that the male deer fight or spar in order to mate. Ancient man noted this behavior and imitated it in an effort to be as powerful as the animals he hunted. And, even today, it is not unheard of for a man or a school boy to fight another in an attempt to impress a woman or school girl with his superior strength and power.

It is for this reason that cave paintings like the "Wizard" depicts a man dressed in the hide, head, and antlers of a stag in a ceremony on the walls of the cave. The depiction of a man wearing horns was linked to the power those horns bestowed upon him. The original polytheistic beliefs were likely those that deified the sexual duality found in nature, the male and female of all species that propagated the continuance of the animal herds that men and women depended upon for protein. Therefore, we can reason that after his religion evolved from animism into polytheism, early man's chief deities became a god and a goddess: the horned god of the hunt and the goddess of fertility—both primarily at the earliest times being concerned with the propagation animals. Later, after hunting and gathering led to rudimentary horticulture and finally to agriculture, the goddess, sometimes depicted with horns herself, became more involved with the fertility of the fields and less so with the fertility of the stalls. The god then became a horned one, and because the sun was the larger of the two most prominent heavenly bodies discernible from earth and the male of the human species was the larger sex, the horned god also became associated with the sun and daylight, while the goddess, likewise, became associated with the moon and the night. Thus, the dual deities united three of the dichotomies in nature into the two deities: day and night, male and female, and the sun and moon. It is likely that each of these dualities was worshipped or petitioned by earlier peoples as individual gods or goddesses as part of the societies' many animistic deities. It seems, then, that the agrarian society with its more sophisticated and complex economy caused a simplification or consolidation in the way people worshiped.

By the 14th Century, the Christian church had ingrained itself into the pagan belief structure by adopting pagan celebrations and holy days, which of course meant that meeting on or about these same times simply made it easier for those of the Old Religion to continue their worship in the ways of the new religion. The holidays now had a different impetus but were held on the same dates. The reasons for these meetings had changed from a pagan one to a Christian one, but that was the main difference. The Christians had included Mary, who in the mind of some took the place of the goddess, and Jesus was the personification of the sacrificed god who had risen from the dead. He was called the Son, but there really was not much difference in the sound of the "Son" of God or the "Sun" of God. This was especially important, I think, because most medieval people were illiterate—they would have needed to be literate in order to recognize the difference.

With the political power of the church structure and a thousand year period in which to convert the pagans, Christianity became ingrained into medieval society. Pagans had always been targeted because their gods were considered false, and the Christians were admonished to have no other gods before them. We have previously discussed the fines and corporal punishments inflicted on those who practiced the Old Way. Since forceful action was taken by the Church against those thought to be witches and heretics, notably in Spain, France, Germany, and the British Isles, the charge of witchcraft was leveled at many of them. They were said to be worshipping Satan. To this end, the Devil was frequently described as having cloven feet (like the god Pan or the Fauns of Dionysis) and horns (like Osirus and Isis or the old horned green god of the English woods, Cernnunos). The Devil was said to attend the Sabbaths in the guise of a goat, probably a man wearing the hide, head, and horns of a goat, and the witches' Sabbath became the "black mass." The meal served during these old religious gatherings became a parody of the sacrament of Eucharist. Thus, the Old Horned God became the Devil, with goat-like cloven hoofs and tail, finally evolving into a long curling tail tipped with a pointed triangle. He became the ruler of hell, carrying a trident like the god Neptune. To one degree or another, evidence leans toward there not being an Old Testament tradition of the Satan, and the modern concept of the Devil is actually a medieval creation based on the combined appearance of the old gods. This Devil, Satan, ruled over hell, where all those that worshipped him were destined to be sent to suffer an eternity of torment in the after-life.

Was hell also a medieval creation? The earliest Biblical reference to hell is in the book of Deuteronomy 32: 22, and it gives the most descriptive depiction of hell in the Old or New Testaments: "For a fire is kindled in my anger, and I shall burn unto the lowest hell, and shall consume the earth with her increase, and set on fire the foundations of the mountains."

Verse 23, which immediately follows, states: "I will heap mischiefs upon them; I will spend mine arrows upon them." The next verse, 24, further states: "*They shall be* burnt with hunger, and devoured with burning heat, and with bitter destruction: I will also send the teeth of beasts upon them with the poison of serpents of the dust."[31] These three verses come from the "Song of Moses," where Moses tells his people about coming to the promised land of Canaan, given by God to the Israelites and which he will be allowed to see but not enter. God was provoked to jealousy by the Israelites worshiping false gods and sacrificing to devils, not to God. He then described in the aforementioned verses what he would do. While this description of hell is certainly not a good one, it does raise in my mind, at least, the notion that this could be interpreted as a place of hell, or as the earth made into a hell. The other references, with the exception perhaps of 2 Samuel 22: 6, "The sorrows of hell compassed me about; the snares of death prevented me; (The 7th verse continues) in my distress I called upon the Lord, and cried to my God: and he did hear my voice out of his temple, and my cry did enter his ears".[32] The next several verses describe the earth shaking and upheavals, smoke and fire. 2 Samuel 22 is a psalm of thanksgiving for the miraculous deliverances God can make and his manifold blessings. The remaining references indicate a place one may be sent for not obeying God's commandments and a place out of the light or presence of God. Arthur Weigall writes that the Christianity of Jesus Christ does not emphasize the wrath of God or His infliction of punishment but sees mainly His love and His unlimited forgiveness of man's frailty.[33] "Indeed, the whole conception of a place of torment where the wicked shall be punished with physical pain and of a wrathful God who is a sort-of combined policeman, magistrate, gaoler [jailer], and executioner cannot be traced to the thoughts of Jesus but belongs to the primitive age and is entirely unworthy of our modern intelligence. Hell, so far as one can interpret the teaching of Jesus, was simply an Outer Darkness, the exclusion from the Kingdom of God, a state of mind, wherein that worm conscience never rested and fires of remorse were not quenched."[34] Christianity has concerned itself so much with this mythical Devil, with the fiery furnace, and with man's escape from it through the atoning sacrifice of Jesus upon the cross and has advocated so continually the worship of Jesus as God and Savior that it has detached the attention of its members from the fact that the mission of the faith should really be the furtherance of the Kingdom of God on earth, the establishment of right living conditions amongst living men.[35] Considering all of the above, I believe that hell and the Devil were devices, albeit with some Biblical mention, that were largely embellished and included in the Bible in order to stop the worship of the pagan deities.

Witches were said to attend a Sabbath or meeting of a coven of twelve witches. Could this be a parody of Jesus and his disciples or King Arthur and his knights or both? The coven leader was sometimes called Arte [*Note: Arte could reference Arthur or the Devil*] and will sometimes appear as a tall, dark man or as a goat. The idea that the Devil might appear as a goat may suggest a priest of the cult wearing an animal mask and or hide. At the Sabbath, the witches would swear allegiance to the Devil. Kissing him under the tail while he was in the guise of a goat was required of the witches. Witches were believed to fly on broomsticks and to possess a flying ointment, one of the ingredients of which was the rendered fat of babies. At the Sabbath, there was a parody of the Catholic Mass. The witches would cast spells that would cause crops to wither and animals to die. Babies were said to be boiled in a cauldron and eaten, and the witches drank a potent witches' brew and danced far into the night before flying back to their homes on a broomstick. All of this sounds pretty fantastical and unbelievable. If we take these matters as true, then witches did all of these things. If, however, they are largely untrue, as I suspect, we may find some grain of truth hidden within them. Lucy Mair points out that certain universal fantasy attributes of the witch are attached to the adherents of minority religions, notably the murder of children, not only for cannibal feasts but also to use parts of their bodies for sorcery. This was the accusation made against Christians by the Jews when they were a heretical sect of the Jews; it was also made against the Jews by Christians.[36] Romans considered Christians to be cannibals because of the wording of the Eucharist: "This is my body, eat of it, and this is the cup of my blood, drink of it, and do this in remembrance of me." To someone spying or listening and not in the know, the wrong assumption could easily be made.

I find it interesting to read what Raymond Buckland wrote about the *Malleus Malificarum*: "Who were the authors of this infamous work? They were two Dominicans, named Jakob Sprenger and Heinrich (Institor) Kramer, Chief Inquisitors for Germany."[37] The appearance of the *Maleus Malificarum* was, in effect, the signal for the persecutions to begin in earnest. As Robbins says, "It opened the flood gates of the inquisitional hysteria."[38] These men wrote the book that kept them in business.

There are some truths in most of the descriptions of the Witches' Sabbath. During Iron Age times and up to the medieval period, there were people of the Old Religion, whether or not they were witches, who used a riding pole in a fertility dance. The pole was ridden hobby-horse fashion, held between the legs. This was definitely a form of phallic symbolism. The members present rode their poles in a great circle, leaping as high in the air as they could. The higher they leapt, the higher the crops were supposed to grow, a clear example of sympathetic magic. These poles that some call wands or Condon, were decorated with carvings and designs. They were easily recognizable and were collected as evidence in witchcraft trials. For this reason, the members of the Old Religion began using broomsticks instead, because everyone had a broom. It is not hard to imagine a group of women jumping around a great circle at night on brooms, as spied by peasants who were afraid and highly superstitious, to be interpreted as witches flying or riding on a broomstick.

The witches did have flying ointments, and a few old recipes exist today, but they contain hallucinatory drugs like aconite, belladonna, or nightshade, which might well give the person using it a euphoric feeling of flying. I suppose, one way or the other, they were taking a trip. There was absolutely no doubt that there was eating and drinking at these meetings, but there was not likely to be cannibalism nor a parody of the Eucharist. The animists and polytheist sometimes sacrificed humans, but victims were not eaten. Could children have been sacrificed? I suppose. But those condemned to death were still being hanged at the crossroads, so why bother? All of these people knew the use of herbs and herbal lore. They were often the real doctors of the time since the learned doctors were not far removed from butchers. As for a blasphemous parody of the Catholic tradition of the Eucharist, I find that unlikely to have happened. It seems ludicrous to me that pagans of the Old Religion, who presumably did not believe in the Eucharist, would mock that tradition; however, there may however been other considerations.

Before leaving the subject of the Eucharist, let's look at some history. There are several sacraments and particular days of observance that have changed or been added over time that were not just traditional Christian observances. Among the sacraments were the Eucharist, baptism, atonement, being washed in the blood, and death and resurrection, the date of Christmas, the Sunday Sabbath, the birthday of Christ, and the resetting of the original date of Christ's birth, seemed to have caused some confliction within the church itself. A number of religions had similar sacraments. Judaism practiced baptism and celebrated Passover on or about the Vernal Equinox. Mithraism practiced a sprinkling of blood from a sacrificed bull and washed with water as a baptism rite designed to wash away sin. Mithra was supposed to have been born in a cave, and that cave was later to be called the birthplace of Jesus. Even the temple hill of the Vatican was a location of a former temple of Mithra. Being washed in the blood of the sacrificial lamb of Judaism is the same idea.

The Eucharist, or the Lord's Supper, likely happened two days before Passover, perhaps Thursday, April 6, in the year A.D. 30. Jesus eats His last meal with His disciples, but now He knows that His death awaits Him unless He takes flight.[39] Yet rather than abandon His mission, He decides to be faithful to the truth that is in Him, even if it leads Him to the grave. He knows now that His kingdom of the Messiah is not of this world. His company was gathered to eat the traditional Passover meal. Jesus knew that He could be arrested at any moment, and His execution would follow as a matter of course. Therefore, when in the usual manner of a host, He handed round pieces of bread to be dipped as sops into the gravy of the cooked lamb, He made the sad remark that even so His body would be broken. And later on after the meal, when, as was customary, He handed round the cup of wine, He likened it to His blood that was to be shed and asked his friends not to forget the sacrifice He was making and to remember His death whenever they broke bread or drank wine.[40] The first century Christian celebration was simply a ceremony of "remembrance" forming part of a real meal, the second element in those days being wine. But in the second century, the ceremony became a sacrament, and at the same time, water took the place of wine. The earliest-known reference to the Christian ceremony is in St. Paul's 1 Corinthians, written some twenty-five years after the Crucifixion. Here, we are told the faithful were wont to meet and to celebrate the Lord's Supper by eating a meal together, apparently from a common stock of provisions, but this had degenerated into an unseemly affair in which some ate or drank too much or too quickly, and others did not get enough. St. Paul therefore enjoins them to restrain themselves and to wait for one another, adding that since it is a sacred meal, in which the body of Jesus is to be discerned, those who are hungry should have something to eat at home before coming.[41] And he warns the Corinthians against participating in similar ceremonies in honor of pagan gods, whom he describes as "devils": "Ye cannot drink the cup of the Lord," he says, "and the cup of devils. Do we want to provoke the Lord to jealousy?"[42] So, we can see from St. Paul that there were parallel ceremonies of Christian and pagan religions going on at the same time. This also manifested itself with regard to Sunday being the Sabbath and when the Lord's birthday was moved from January 6 to December 25. I think the Christian Church was broadening its appeal to bring people to the Lord and make it easier for them to convert.

It seems to me that Murray had some things right and the witch hysteria, especially in Salem, may have had nothing to do with witchcraft. And the preponderance of the evidence seems to point to the notion that, while some Neolithic traditions lasted into the Middle Ages, whether these traditions have anything to do with witchcraft is more or less tenuous, unless of course Murray is correct. I think anyone that believes the way the inquisitors Sprenger and Kramer did probably still believe in the Easter Bunny and the Tooth Fairy, which leaves the original question—"What is, or was, witchcraft?"—unanswered.

There is, of course, Mair's proposition that in spite of what modern devotees state about having to be initiated to be a witch, there is a fourth possibility that the practice, power, or whatever else it is called, can be passed down through genetics, heredity, or through natural talents and abilities. Leah Smock, Marie Laveau, and others may have been hereditary witches, either inheriting the traits or being carefully groomed and taught the healing occult lore. But I think there is yet another possibility.

I am going to offer a new hypothesis that may shine more light on the subject, although it is also unproven. I think Margaret A. Murray was close but not completely there. Certainly, archaeological evidence shows that some Neolithic traditions persisted until at least the 14th century and may exist in places even today. The religious beliefs and practices of those considered witches inclusive of herbal lore, the ability to cause a mental or physical change in anything through the use of sympathetic magic, intuition, second sight, or other means, was enough to validate that consideration. You could, of course, call them faith (or folk) healers, water witches (dowsers), midwives, or herb doctors. Many of the old people in Kentucky still hang onto the family cures and traditions handed down from generation to generation. Often, these people seem to have the ability to look into the minds and hearts of those around them and seem to know what they are thinking. Others know the right signs to plant by and when to dig fence post holes or clear brush based on when the stars say it's best. Still others know the plants that grow in the woods and fields and what to do with them to effect cures.

My Grandmother Fischer could remove warts from the hands of her neighbors. In the practical sense, doesn't this ability fulfill the role of the wise woman in the shires of England or villages of other Western Europe? Does it matter they go to Anglican, Baptist, Catholic, Episcopal, and Methodist Churches, as well as mosques, Jewish temples, and other houses of worship? Our economy developed into the most complex, complicated, and sophisticated the world has ever seen, animism and polytheism no longer work well for us. We have one God because we have economically, socially, and, finally, spiritually evolved to that point. To be sure, there is a dichotomy in nature: day and night, male and female, good and evil, love and hate, yin and yang, and death and resurrection. We should be aware, however, that there are less sophisticated societies that continue to need a variety of deities to accommodate their spiritual requirements, as we once did.

My definition of witchcraft does not lie with Neolithic traditions or people riding broomsticks, stirring cauldrons, or dancing in circles. My witches or wise ones know the use of herbs and the signs that are important to our health and well-being. They have a knowledge that goes beyond the natural order of things and possess an intuition. They know the star signs and are superstitious. They may use bottles, jars, candles and wax above what everyday usage requires. These people dry herbs for use in the winter and employ mortars and pestles for their processing. Without calling themselves witches, they may be perceived as such because of what they do. These people know how to heal and make medicine. They are familiar with flora and fauna, and they keep the important superstitions alive. Perception can become reality. I was once told that perception can be your best friend or your worst enemy. It may have been this perception that killed Leah Smock.

Chapter 6
THE OLD WAYS COME
TO THE NEW WORLD

The "Old Ones" were the wise people of medieval Europe. Later, some of these people moved to the colonies, but probably not many due to their advanced age and the cost involved. Most if not all of the old wise ones, realizing the nature of things, tried to pass their knowledge on to someone younger before they died. It is those younger people who may have made it to the colonies, albeit with some, but likely not all, of the ancient lore.

A Word about Modern Wicca

Some sincere neo-pagans, and perhaps some with less noble intent, use the word wicca to validate themselves as witches. The double "C" is pronounced "CH," like in Italian. The word wica, with one "C," is an old Anglo-Saxon word, meaning a "wise one".[43] If you pronounce wicca using the "CH" sound it comes out wicha, or, the purported origin of the word, "witch." When looking up the etymology of the word "wicca," one finds reference to "wicce" and "wicca," meaning diviner or soothsayer. Robert Graves states that willow, or osier, in Greece was sacred to Hecate, Circe, Hera, and Persephone, all death aspects of the Triple Moon Goddess and much worshipped by witches: "It's, willow or wei, connection with witches is so strong in northern Europe, that the words witch and wicked are from the same ancient word for willow which also yields wicker.[44] We do know the passage from the Bible "suffer not a witch to live" was originally "suffer not a poisoner to live." The original word was *venefica* (meaning poisoner), rather than *malefica* (witch).[45] It was changed in the King James translation. I think it more likely that since King James was footing the bill for the translation of the Bible, an expensive proposition, the wording was changed to make it easier for him to govern his people.

European Witch Lore and the connection to Leah Smock

The real "wise ones" of today are more often Christian and attend church on a regular basis; they are elderly or aging, rural, and respected. Some spend much of their time out-of-doors and in the woods. My Grandfather Bryant called such people "woodsy." It is interesting to me that the arcane knowledge and psychic, intuitive, or natural ability these folks have seems to be split up amongst them. Years before in the old country, they might have each possessed an overall knowledge, but realizing that some would be better at certain things than others, they became specialists. For example, those that know about planting by the signs may not have the same level of knowledge about herbs that the herbalist has. Some healers can remove the pain from a burn victim, while others may be able to cure the thrush. Still others cannot do any of that but can make a wart go away or make medicines and poultices to heal. I suspect that when people were closer to the Earth, with fewer conveniences, they learned more.

In 1966, a novice high school teacher took a position at Rabun Gap-Nacoochee School in Georgia. His name was Eliot Wiggenton, and he taught ninth and tenth grade English and geography. Like most teachers, he had lots of duties and wore many hats, and like all new teachers (I was one once), he was lost trying to teach rowdy kids who were bored with his lectures and lessons. One day, he came into the class that was going absolutely nowhere and said, "How would you like to start a magazine?" From that attempt to break through with the class, the beginning of the *Foxfire* books came into being. For those of you unfamiliar with these books, they chronicle the lives of the old Appalachian Mountain people and their arts and industries. Mr. Wiggenton had heard of planting by the signs and didn't know what that meant, but he thought it would be a good topic to put into the magazine. He asked his students, but they did not know what it meant either, so they went home and asked their parents and older relations, and probably for the first time in their lives, they really talked to people other than their peers, having a real conversation. These conversations revealed superstitions, old home remedies, weather signs, and directions for planting by the signs[46]. To be sure, many other topics came to light, and eventually this classroom project designed to get kids from the Appalachian Mountains to participate in class turned into a fifteen volume set of books that are used and enjoyed by thousands and perhaps millions of people. The students not only learned what valuable information these old folks held, but they learned to interview them and take notes so that they could write these stories and share them with others. This project also taught the students to have a pride in their heritage and history. Very often, pride is something hard to find in areas like Appalachia and other areas of my state, Kentucky. The popular press portrays feuds, illegal stills, and bearded, barefoot, illiterate mountaineers as representative of the state, not the rich history and heritage of the pioneers who fought for and settled this rich land. John and Elizabeth Smock were pioneers in this land and brought with them the knowledge taught to Leah. It is from these isolated rural settings that I believe the last vestiges of the "wise ones" continue to exist. And all one has to do is talk to the old folks, and they will share their lifetime of experience. Leah Smock, her parents, and their neighbors made use of this lore because there were no weathermen, scientists, radios, or televisions and few newspapers. They had to be self-reliant. They observed nature and forecasted and planted by what nature predicted.

Weather Signs

Since the wise ones were involved with fertility and needed to predict the weather so that the village could prosper or prepare for hard times, they needed to look to natural signs to foretell the weather. To many people, this appeared to be magic or clairvoyance, but it was simply interpreting observations of nature. I will give several examples of these observations and deductions from them that lead to forecasting the weather.

The winter will be cold if the squirrels grow bushier tails, begin gathering nuts (cutting) in August or early September, and build their nests low in the trees. Abnormally thick hair or fur growth on wild and domestic animals, such as horses, sheep, mules, and cows, also indicate a cold winter. If crows gather together, owls hoot late in the fall or high in the mountains, and birds huddle on the ground or eat all the wild berries, such as the sumacs, early, a cold winter can be expected. If wild hogs gather sticks, straw, and shucks to make their beds or cows' hooves break off earlier, this is a sign of a bad winter. If the deer are abnormally fat and have thick coats, the winter will be hard.

Other signs of a bad winter include the wooly worms: if there are a lot of them crawling about, if they have thicker coats or wider black bands, or if the worm's coat is more black than red, the winter will be cold. If he's brown at both ends and red in the middle, the winter will be mild. It will also be a bad winter if the yellow jackets are heavier and closer to the ground than normal. Three months after the first katydid begins calling, the first killing frost will come. *Note: My niece Melanie, Fran, and I were together at a recent wedding. Melanie was complaining to me about how loud the katydids were at her condo. The first killing frost, by lore, is ninety days after the first Katydid calls. I asked her when they began to call, and she said about two weeks earlier. I had not heard any at that time. I backed up the date to about August 22. I added to that number ninety days, making the date for the first killing frost to be November 20. We had a man by the name of Dick Frymire die in nearby Breckenridge County. Dick was known for his herbal remedies and for being a prognosticator of weather. He has been featured on numerous television shows, such as Johnny Carson, David Letterman and many others. The* Meade County Messenger, *our local newspaper, published his final weather forecast, and he had November 19 as the first killing frost. Is this a coincidence? I don't think so.* When butterflies migrate early, winter will be earlier, and when they begin bunching together in the air, winter is coming soon.

It will be a bad winter if sweet potatoes have a thicker skin, onions have more layers, carrots grow deeper, and blackberry blooms are especially heavy. If the trees are heavily laden with green leaves late in the fall or if the acorn crop is heavy and the dogwood and holly berries are heavy the winter will be bad. The darker green the grass is in the summer, the colder it will be in the winter. It will be a cold winter if the smoke from the chimney flows downward or settles on the ground. When you build a fire outside in the winter and it pops more than usual, there will be a snow in three days. If it's cloudy and the smoke readily rises, there is a chance of snow. Two frosts and lots of rain mean a cold winter. If the first frost is late, the winter will be hard. If the first snow stays on the ground more than three days, there will be another snow that covers it. The hotter the summer is, the colder the winter.

It will rain if the leaves turn their backs and the trees look mottled. *Actually, biology confirms this effect. Trees take water from two sources, the taproots and the back of their leaves. The trees turn their leaves to absorb water.* If the points of the moon are down or the cows lay down in the pasture, it means rain. If there is a ring around the moon, count the stars in the ring and that will be how many days it will be until it rains. If you see a black snake in a tree, it will rain within three days. If the birds fly low to the ground, it will rain. If it rains on the three longest days of the year (one day on either side of the summer solstice), the acorn mast will be low, predicting a mild winter.

Obviously, all of the signs that foretell weather don't happen consistently and concurrently with each other all of the time. But when a preponderance of the signs coincide, the chances are good that the weather they portend will come to pass, more often than not.

The Planetary Signs

Thirty thousand years ago, man began to learn about the heavens from watching the stars and, with the use of rudimentary calculations, discovered the solstices and the equinoxes. I taught these to my history, geography, and social studies students. They are simple and very important to planting times and animal husbandry and are used even today by fish and game departments when setting hunting seasons. Ancient people did not have a fish and game department, so they had to learn by themselves. It happened that there were seven "planets" known to ancient astronomy–the sun, the moon, Mars, Mercury, Jupiter, Venus, and Saturn, and where a seven-day week was in use, there is reason to suppose that the days were dedicated to those planets.[47]

The secret to determining the seasons lies with the way the Earth orbits the sun. The Earth revolves around the sun, while the latter rotates on its axis. Every twenty-four hours, the Earth makes a complete rotation. It takes 365 days for the Earth to make one complete revolution around the sun. During this process, the Earth wobbles slowly to the north for about six months and then begins to wobble slowly south for six months. Midway through this process both ways, the Earth wobbles in such a way that the sun shines directly on the equator. When it is revolving further north, it maximizes the sunshine directly on a line further north and parallel to the equator, the Tropic of Cancer. At this point in the Northern Hemisphere, it is summer. When it continues, it wobbles the other way as far as it can, and the sun will shine directly on the Tropic of Capricorn. Then in the Northern Hemisphere, it is winter. The land between the Tropic of Cancer and Capricorn are considered the tropics.

While this information might at first glance seem interesting but of little value, it is the reason we have seasons, and in every part of the world, people decide when to plant and harvest according to the season. These seasons also affect the mating times and migration of animals. The Kentucky Fish and Wildlife Department actually uses some of this information when setting hunting season dates. The rut, the mating season of deer, begins on the first full moon after the autumnal equinox. This is the time when the does are in small herds and in estrus, and the bucks spar with other males to assemble their harems, usually about five to seven does per buck. This is the optimum time for hunters to be successful. The ancients didn't have a fish and game department to tell them this. They had to calculate it for themselves.

Work and Planting by the Signs

"To everything there is a season, and a time for every purpose under the heaven: a time to be born, and a time to die; a time to plant, and a time to pluck up that which has been planted." Ecclesiastes 3:1-2

Ancient astronomers discovered that a number of the bright constellations of stars they studied and named were evenly spaced along the yearly path of the sun in a belt about eighteen degrees wide. This belt also included the paths of the planets and the monthly path of the moon. This belt was subsequently divided into twelve parts, each thirty degrees in length, called "signs." Each of these signs contained a constellation of stars, and each sign thus received its name from the name of the constellation it contained. Since all the signs except Libra were named after living things, the belt was named the Zodiac or "zone of animals."[48] A way of planting by the signs is described in the *Foxfire* books."

The proper use of this information is prescribed differently, but in general there are some things that have to do with the moon that should be coupled with the general rules. The moon exacts an influence over the tides, the bloodstream, and even human behavior. Oftentimes, when I was teaching school, the students would become rowdier and bouncing off the walls for no apparent reason; invariably someone would comment, "It's a full moon!" Often enough, that person was correct. I had a friend who worked in a mental hospital, and she also noticed an accelerated frantic behavior in the patients during the full moon and a few days leading up to it. Another friend was in law enforcement and noted that arrests increased a few days before the full moon culminated. Teachers, police, doctors, and nurses all have noted the lunar effect.

When I was in New York in 1965 and spent time talking with the English couple and some of their friends, I was told something about what they called moon magic. It comes down to gauging or planning what you do depending on the moon phase. After the dark of the moon, last phase waning, the moon begins to grow for about a fortnight (two weeks). This time is not propitious for getting a haircut, cutting your grass, trimming the hedges, weed eating, or almost anything else like that because the hair, grass, hedges, and weeds will grow faster during a waxing moon. Haircuts will last longer when obtained during a waning moon, up to about two weeks after a full moon. *The origin of the seven day week, which was used by the Jews and certain other peoples but not till later by the Greeks or Romans, is to be sought in some primitive worship of the moon, for the custom of keeping the day of the new moon and that of the full moon festivals, which is widely found in antiquity, implies the recognition of a cycle of fourteen days, of which a week is half, the actual length of a week thus determined being 7 3/8 days.*[49] *The length of a lunar month is about twenty-eight days, or a full moon cycle. Because of the 3/8 of a day, occasionally there will be two full moons in a month. The "Blue Moon" is the second full moon in any month. A Blue Moon occurs about once every three years. (The old saying "once in a blue moon" means not very often.)* You will not have to shave as often on a waning moon nor will the grass grow as fast, meaning less cutting and gasoline cost. Of course, this holds true for weed eating, etc. Now, this appears to be magic of a sympathetic sort, but it really is just observing what happens in nature and using it to your advantage. The old wise ones knew these things because they lived closer to nature.

Planting by the signs has some rules as well, and they go beyond planting. Each sign is known as being either masculine or feminine. They are also known to be airy, dry, barren, fiery, earthy, moist, watery, fruitful, or very fruitful. In general, any activity that requires a dry atmosphere, such as painting, should be done in the dry signs, and any activity requiring moisture, such as some planting, should be done on one of the moist or fruitful signs. The best time of all, of course, falls on both an ideal sign and a good phase of the moon.

Planting is best done in the fruitful signs of Scorpio, Pisces, and Taurus, when the signs are in the loins, feet, neck, or breast. Plow, till, and cultivate in Aires. Never plant anything in the barren signs, as they are best for trimming, deadening, and destroying. Graft just before sap starts to flow in the spring and while the moon is in its first or second quarter (waxing). Always set plants out in a water or earth sign. Never plant in the heart or head, as these are death signs, and when the moon is waning, plant things that will yield above the ground. In the last quarter of the waning moon, pull weeds, weed eat, turn sod, till, and remove brush. The old people knew this, but the people that plant by the signs now are slowly dying off and, unfortunately, with them dies the lore.

There is much more to this and many more rules, but to illustrate the things that the old people did to ensure the fertility of plants and animals, these examples will suffice. It is probable that the Smocks utilized this knowledge. They were noted for taking a poor patch of ground and growing wonderful produce. The Smocks knew the use of herbs and made remedies. The Smocks, as were all people, superstitious.

Chapter 7

SUPERSTITIONS AND
FOLK HEALERS

S uperstition is defined by *Webster's New World Dictionary* and *Roget's Thesaurus* as Groundless belief in supernatural agencies; a popular belief held without reason.[50] This is pretty much a typical definition, generally correct but not specifically. Sometimes, the belief has a reason; for example, it is bad luck to walk under a ladder, but that superstition is grounded in good common sense. If you walk under a ladder, you could trip and fall against it and knock the person on the ladder to the ground. That would be bad luck for him. Or the person on the ladder could drop a tool, paint brush, bucket of paint, or himself/herself onto you. Bad luck for you. So, the dictionary definition does not always serve us well. Another more reasonable definition is Unreasoning awe or fear of something unknown, mysterious, or imaginary; a tenet, scruple, habit, etc. founded on fear or ignorance.[51] I would add to this definition the clause: "That causes a behavioral change." The belief in superstition sometimes causes people to change their behavior in an overt way, such as throwing a pinch of spilt salt over one's shoulder, or in a covert way, such as avoiding stepping on a grave or walking under a ladder. Some of these things make sense if looked at objectively, while others aren't so clear.

There are superstitions with which many people are not familiar. When I was little, my mother would not let me walk with one shoe on and one off. She said it was bad luck. Once a bird almost came in the front door and Mom shooed it out; she said a bird in the house was bad luck because someone would die. I guess everyone knows that the left hind foot of a rabbit brings luck in the same way a four-leaf clover does. Whenever we found a penny, Mom told us to put it in our shoe. That was supposed to bring luck. I once had a friend who also believed that finding a penny was good luck, but he thought that it had to be heads up, and it didn't go in his shoe but rather his pocket. I always thought that their family was better off than ours. We didn't discriminate between heads or tails, a penny found was a penny gained, even if you had to walk on it the rest of the day. Of course, they didn't know that and probably spent the penny. I saw a horseshoe nailed above a door on a farm house in Drake, Kentucky, for luck. Papa Bryant said it was wrong—the points or ends of the shoe were not up. Because it had been nailed in reverse, all the luck ran out and it did no good. Mom always said things ran in threes, and she pointed out enough examples when I was growing up that I was, and still am, convinced they often do. If salt is spilt, one has to throw a pinch over the left shoulder. A broken mirror will bring seven years' bad luck. I don't know how many mirrors I have broken, and it either accounts for my life, which has been pretty good but could have been a lot better had they not been broken or if the bad luck didn't come; however, I understand that mirrors used to be very costly, and it might take seven years to save enough to get another, causing a sacrifice in other necessities to obtain a replacement. Don't step on a grave because it is bad luck. Maybe it is, but I think it shows disrespect and bad manners. There are many superstitions that were believed and respected by all early pioneers and their descendants even until today. If one was not sure, why take a chance?

Folk Healers and Remedies

Before I begin relating any remedies or telling of methods the folk healers have employed, let me state unequivocally that neither the author nor the publisher recommend any readers try these remedies. No guarantees of their efficacy are implied or recommended; they are simply listed as examples of things that have happened in the author's families or reportedly in that of other families.

My father suffered a third degree burn when he was about four years old. Under his left arm, he was terribly burned on both his arm and left side. He was badly scarred. When I was a toddler, I used to crawl in the bed with Dad and sleep on his arm. I thought that was the best thing in the world, and I seldom felt safer. My Dad was a handsome man and a veteran of Okinawa. He sailed on the battleships *Nevada* and *Iowa*. He had been a professional boxer during the Depression. He was firm, gentle but fierce, when it came to protecting his family. One day, I asked Dad about his burn, and he simply told me he got burned when he was a child. When I was with my grandmother Fischer—I called her Mamaw—I asked her how Dad had gotten burned so badly. She told me that he had a flannel gown on and toddled too close to the red-hot potbelly stove, and his clothes caught fire. She said that it was in doubt that he would live but live he did. The pain was so bad that he cried continuously until he passed out from exhaustion, only to awaken and continue screaming from the pain. The pain could not be moderated. Then she told me a secret. The doctor said if he didn't get some rest, he would die of exhaustion. She was told about a neighbor who could take away the pain from a burn, and my Grandmother Fischer went to see her. The woman came to the house and laid her hands on Dad while whispering something inaudible. She said he would sleep comfortably because she took away his pain, and he would be all right.

I thought that was a funny story and did not believe it happened. I thought she was telling me a tale. So, when I got home from my visit, I told Dad about what she said, and I laughed. Dad told me that it wasn't a story and that I shouldn't laugh about it. He said that, even though he was a toddler, he could remember the pain leaving him and the relief it brought. He said, "Gerry, it was the first time in weeks that I slept."

Mamaw told me something else. She said that she asked the woman, after Dad went instantly to sleep, how much had her child suffered? She held out her arm and told Mamaw to take hold of it, which she did. Instantly, she recoiled in pain. She said the woman's arm felt like red-hot iron. I was a mere boy, but even at that age, I knew the story was true. Two of the people I trusted most in the world told me so. My grandmother asked the lady if she could teach her to take the pain away if it became necessary. She said no. She could teach others, but it had to be woman to man and then man to woman. It could not be taught woman to woman. This incident happened in Decatur, Alabama, sometime in 1925 or 1926.

In the Appalachians, there are still people who are able to heal by faith. People today are skeptical of faith healers, likely because of commercial televangelists who ask for money. There is another reason. We have grown up in an age and society that taught us to believe superstition is nonsense and science is not. Eliot Wiggenton says, The elderly healers with whom we talked are quiet, simple, strong, and sure. They are people with a faith of such quality that the differences between us and them were abundantly clear. They have faith in themselves and they have faith in their God, believing that it is through Him their words carry weight. They do not heal in tents. They do not cry out over radios. They do not accept money for their work. They help their neighbors, and neighbors' children when asked to help, and they respond as a gesture of friendship and concern.[52]

There are generally three categories of healers with some exceptions: those that can ease the pain of burns, allowing time for accepted medical cures to work; those that can stop bleeding; and those that can cure thrush. Some of the healers can heal all three of the aforementioned afflictions, and some, like the woman that drew the fire from my dad's arm, only one.

Wiggenton describes the people his class interviewed as those who can blow or draw the fire from the burn. One elderly woman who could do all three types of healings stated that she didn't have to touch the person; she just had to talk to the Lord and it's all right: "And when you blow fire, you blow on the burned place and say somethin'—it's out'a the Bible…I can't read. And I can't write. It's just a gift from God. I just commenced at it." Another lady healer, when asked about drawing fire, said, "You blow your breath on it and th' fires gone out." Her method was to pass her hands over the burn three times while gently blowing her breath over it and to repeat slowly the verse each time. Wiggenton writes, as they were getting ready to leave, they thanked her for speaking with them. She answered,

"Well, it might be of some use to you when I'm gone. I believe in th' healin' power because the Lord has healed me… that's the greatest thing they is—the healin' power of the Savior." Another healer stated: "That's why I say lots a'times these things come in better 'cause a doctor couldn't get t'that on the inside a'that thing, and we could because we let our Maker do that. We don't doctor it. Other words, I mean, we don't cure it. We're the vessel for the Lord t'let us do the work, and He does the curin'."[53]

It was interesting to me that one of the male healers said that he could only teach the method to a woman and not to another man. This parallels what the woman that eased Dad's burn said. She could only pass the knowledge on to a man. Those who blew the fire had to be with the patient, but it was not always necessary to be with them when bleeding was stopped. One of the healers who could stop bleeding said the same process for drawing fire was used, except the word "blood" was used in place of "fire". One healer stated that the bleeding could be stopped over the telephone. To cure a hemorrhage, say the following: "As I was walking in Jordon Wood, there was the water and there it stood. So shall thy blood stay in thy body,_____ (name). I do thee bless in the name of the Father, Son, and Holy Ghost."

Curing thrush is something that most all of the healers could do. I admit that I did not know what thrush happened to be, so I looked up the definition in *Webster's Dictionary*: "a disease that is caused by a fungus (Candida albicans) occurs especially in infants and children and is marked by white patches in the oral cavity."[54] I am somewhat familiar with shingles, a virus of the nerves caused by the chickenpox virus that remains in the body long after the original disease is cured. The symptoms described as "the thrush" sound hauntingly similar to shingles. I remember my mother getting shingles several times. The first time it occurred was on her tongue, and it was a small white patch of blisters no larger than a circle of ¼ inch in diameter, but they were so painful she could not eat for days. All of her nutrition came from soups and other liquids. Thrush, from its description, looks much like shingles, although they might not all be the same.

Thrush is described as a patch of blisters in the mouth of children, usually nursing infants, and occasionally on the breasts of their mother's. [Note: This would indicate a contagious fungal disease.] The blisters are painful, and the babies can't feed, or in the case of the mothers, the babies can't feed and the mothers can't breastfeed their children. There are four types described by the healers—white, red, yellow, and black. The type is diagnosed by the color of the blisters. This condition was mentioned by all of the healers Wiggenton and his class interviewed.

One of the healers called it "thrash," and when asked how he cured it, he responded that "he didn't know." Some healers seem to blow their breath over the infected area, and others cup their hand over it and blow it away. Some of them recite a verse. There is a disparity in the means that the faith healers use, but the common denominator is their faith in Jesus and the Bible. Wiggenton states that he was given three different verses by three faith healers. The effect, then, is not just the words but the faith of the healer. I suppose it's not what you say but the faith that does the healing. One Bible verse supposedly used by a healer is from the sixteenth chapter of Ezekiel.

"And when I passed by *thee*, and saw thee polluted in thine own blood, I said unto *thee when thou wast* in thy blood, Live; yea, I said unto *thee when thou wast* in thy blood, Live."

The only requirement is to substitute the person's full name each time "thou" or "thee" appear.[55] Another old way for burns and scalds to remove the pain is to repeat the following verse: "Three ladies come from the coast, one with fire and two with frost. Out with thee, fire, and in with the frost. In the name of the Father, Son, and Holy Ghost."

There are other healers that cure, or claim to cure, other afflictions or take away pain. My Grandmother Fischer could do this. She learned as a girl in Alabama to take away warts. When people found out about it, they would send their children to her or come themselves when they woke up to find a wart. She would tell the people to bring a used wash-cloth, and when they came, she would carefully wipe the cloth over the wart several times and then tell the person to go home and bury the cloth under the back porch or the back porch steps. When the cloth was buried, the wart would disappear as the former rotted away. This is a case of sympathetic magic. She wiped the object to be gone, although no one knew back then she imbued it with the essence of the wart. Then, as the wart essence dissolved, the wart vanished. I suspect the essence, if that was part of the operation, has a very short life span when buried because the wart was gone in three or four days or sometimes a week. In Decatur, Alabama, she was quite popular for this ability, and as a child, I remember one time when she did this for a neighbor.

One medieval method for removing warts that sounds a little more witch-like goes like so: Take a snail and rub it on the wart. Then, impale the snail with a thorn. As the snail wastes away, so shall the wart. My wife, as a child, had a seed wart grow or attach itself to her thumb. Her father, who was from Pennsylvania, took a piece of bacon and rubbed the wart and buried the bacon. Within a few days, the wart went away. Another medieval wart removal method is to stick a pin in a Roman tree. (Mountain Ash)

I have met two women who had what they called "healing hands." One of the women was a lady in New York City who used her gift or talent to relieve the pain of sunburns, leg cramps, menstrual pain, and the like. She could also lower fevers by standing behind or in front of the patient, carefully placing her hands on each side of the patient's head and drawing her hands toward herself. Once her hands were no longer touching the patient, she would perform what she called "shake them off." This was a downward motion, much like shaking off water from your hands. This motion was supposed to get the pain, fever, or whatever the affliction was off her hands before she repeated the procedure. She continued to do this for several minutes until she felt no need to do it any longer. I also watched her test another woman by blindfolding her and having her hold out her hands, palms up. The lady who had the healing hands would place both hands over and under the blindfolded lady's hand. She would ask, "Where are my hands now?" Each time, the woman answered correctly. Later, she would change the procedure where only one hand was above or below that of the one being tested. The tested lady continued to state correctly, "Above my left hand, below my right hand, over both, under both." It was truly impressive. When she was finished with the testing, the lady with the healing hands took the blindfold from the eyes of the one being tested and proclaimed to her that she also had the gift. The lady who was tested and found worthy used her hands in much the same way with her children, easing sunburns and minor afflictions.

To me at least, faith healers seem to have a gift that is either innate or God-given to cure and ease pain through their faith. The strength of these people seems to lie in two essential matters: firstly, their belief or faith in God and secondly, faith in themselves. It seems problematic to me that one of these can exist in someone and not the other; however, some very faithful and God-fearing people cannot heal while others can. And some people who are healers are not Christian.

Chapter 8
HERBS AND REMEDIES

Some Common Herbs

I am going to warn the readers at the outset of this chapter that any of the remedies listed should not be taken or prescribed to others without making sure that the person taking the remedy is not allergic to any of the ingredients or combination of them. I also warn readers that, while you may not be allergic to any of these herbal remedies or ingredients, these ingredients may react in a negative way to prescribed medicines you may be taking. The best rule before trying anything in this chapter is to consult with your doctor before doing so. None of the herbs or combinations of them are toxic themselves, unless taken in extremely high doses or unless one is allergic to them. Most of these herbs and chemicals are safely used in cooking, but for some people, they can be dangerous alone or in combination. Use caution and consult your doctor before taking. Above all, allow anything you boil to cool to room temperature before applying to any part of the body.

I have safely used many of these remedies with success. Some I have never tried. Some my mother and father used on me to reduce the pain of earaches or bee stings. Still others were used by my Grandmother Bryant on her family or my Great-Grandmother Koeth's family. Providing they are safe for you or others to use (it is your responsibility to make sure), they are a lot of fun, and they may have the desired result.

You will note that many ingredients are used repeatedly, such as apple cider vinegar, mint, honey, and chamomile. Other ingredients, such as coal oil (today called kerosene), turpentine, and whiskey, are also used. It is not recommended that one drink kerosene or turpentine, but people did use these ingredients, one way or another, from time to time.

When I was a child, we used coal oil lamps on the farm. Electricity was not available. Coal oil was what we burned, and it was denser and oilier than today's kerosene. They are not exactly the same. I am taking these remedies largely from my own collection of herbal medicines, as well as other sources. These remedies have been used for hundreds and perhaps thousands of years. Since there are thousands of remedies, I will relate only the ones that involve common ailments treated with common ingredients. We grow in our herb gardens, basil, chives, oregano, mint, rosemary, sage, thyme, and violets. Poke, may apple, hazelnut, wild strawberry, burdock, elm, hickory, walnut, willow, oak, maple, juniper, chicory, goldenrod, honeysuckle, mulberry, wild garlic (onion), sumac, dandelion, blackberry, and elderberry grow all around my yard. I can remember my Grandmother Bryant cutting herbs in her yard to make a remedy or to get some root or leaf to put a taste in the food she cooked. I will list a number of common plants and liquids, and where possible, I will give information about the plant and, for those interested in planting or usage according to the signs of its planet.

Medicinal Roots, Herbs, Barks, and Liquids

Aniseed (*Anisi Semina*) (*Pimpinella anisum*): Anise has a licorice flavor. It has been used in baking, cooking, and in flavoring of alcohol. It is governed by Jupiter, and it is used as a digestive aid, to soothe dyspepsia, colic, and gas. It is also used in breaking up congestion and as an ingredient in cough syrups. Anise can be purchased at most any supermarket.

Birch Tree (*Betula Alba*): This tree is under the dominion of Venus and is a diuretic. The juice of young leaves, the distilled water of them, or the sap produced by boring a hole in the tree is good for dropsy, scurvy, and all cutaneous ailments. A strong decoction of the leaves is good to soothe sore mouths, aids the kidneys, and breaks up kidney stones.

Burdock *(Arctium Lappa)* or *Lappa Minor (A. minus)*: This plant is commonly called the cockleburr. This plant is under the rule of Venus. It produces a burr that attaches itself to clothing and animal hair, which aids in distributing the seed. The root is chiefly used by being boiled or infused in water. It is good for poultices, and the leaves have been used in a poultice by my great-grandmother to draw the venom from my grandfather's arm when he was bitten by a copperhead snake. It can be used for skin conditions, such as acne, boils, rashes, psoriasis, eczema, and dermatitis. It is also used in rheumatism and gout.

Carraway (*Carum Carui*) (*Carum Carvi*): This plant is governed by Mercury. The seed is the principal part of the plant to be used, although the root is edible. The seed, when powdered and mixed as a poultice, will take the blackness from bruises. The seeds are used to soothe stomach pains in children and adults. They ease pain and aid digestion and expel gas or flatulence. Mixed with peppermint oil or mint leaves, it aids digestion and acid reflux.

Cucumber (*Cucumis Sativus*): Cucumber is under the dominion of the moon. The uses for this plant are many. It is a gentle diuretic, good for intestinal health, and helps to lower blood sugar. It is used as an ingredient in cosmetics because of its benefit to the skin. It soothes sunburn and redness and is said to lighten freckles.

Dandelion (*Taraxacum*) (*Taraxacum officinale*): Dandelion is under Jupiter and is good for the blood, acting as an aperient and diuretic. It is good for the liver, jaundice, and stomach complaints. Most diuretics deplete potassium; however, dandelion is high in potassium. Add four ounces of the root to two pints of water, boil gently down to one pint, and then strain while hot. Take three tablespoons six times a day.

Elderberry, Elder Tree (*Sambucus nigra*): The Elder is under Venus. Tea is made from the young leaves and buds. The berries are good for a fever, and two teaspoons full of the juice should be taken. When the leaves are boiled in fat until they are crisp and the fat is green, the result is good for softening callouses, old sores, etc. The berries are used as an anti-inflammatory to soothe coughs, sore throats, and bronchial infections. They also combat viruses and the flu. This can be made into syrup, and it is good for the elderly or very young.

Elm Tree (*Ulmus Campetis*): This tree is ruled by Saturn. The inner bark of this tree is good for herpes, lepra, and itchy legs. Boil four ounces of the inner bark in four pints of water. Boil until the water is reduced to two pints. Take of this a gill twice or three times. *Note: A pound of liquid equals one pound of weight. A gill would then be 4 ounces of weight.* The green leaves of the elm were chewed to ward off hunger and serve as an appetite depressant.

Flax, Common (*Linum Usitatissimum*): Flax is under Saturn. The seeds can be made into poultices, fomentations, and teas. A tea made from its seeds is used for coughs bladder irritation, and disorders of the chest, lungs, and kidneys. A teacupful at any time and a poultice of the bruised seeds is a remedy against parts affected with pain and inflammation, gout, or rheumatism.

Garlic (*Allium Sativum*): Garlic is an herb of Mars. It is used for asthma, hysteria, worms, and scurvy. Extracts of the cloves are natural antiseptics and are used to treat flu, bronchitis, and nasal congestion. It lowers cholesterol and blood pressure. It can be used to treat skin fungi, such as athlete's foot and ringworm, swallowing one to six cloves two or three times a day. You can take a pound of the peeled cloves, extract the juice, and add a pint of water. Next, add a pint of red wine vinegar or milk to the pressed roots allow to macerate for an hour, and then press it out. Afterward, add three pounds of refined sugar. Skim off any impurities, and take one tablespoon.

Golden Rod (*Solidago Virgo*): This plant is a common wildflower under Venus. A tea made from the new leaves makes a licorice-flavored spring tonic. In the form of a decoction or infusion, they have been used for weakness and laxness of the bowels. It is good for stopping internal hemorrhages. One teaspoonful three times a day of a powder made from the dried flowers and green leaves is given in honey or one ounce of the plant in a pint of boiling water.

Mallow (*Malva Sylvestris*): This plant is a member of the mallow family, related to the hibiscus. This herb is used as a skin astringent and for bronchitis, constipation, hoarseness, laryngitis, teething pain, and mouth, throat, and vaginal irritations. Mallow should be avoided if you're pregnant or breastfeeding. Take an infusion orally or eat five grams of the chopped herb daily.

Marigold (*Calendula officnalis*): Marigold is an herb of the Sun under Leo and, therefore, strengthens the heart. When a tea is made from the fresh orange flowers and picked free from the calyx (the combined sepals or bud that holds the bloom), it is good against fevers. It also brings out perspiration, and it brings out anything that ought to appear on the skin, such as measles. It helps minor burns and insect bites. It also aids stomach disorders.

Mint (*Mentha Viridis*): Mint is governed by Venus. Mint will stop vomiting and create an appetite. It is used fresh or dried. It can be used against anorexia. It is best given in simple distilled water or in the form of a tea. It's also really good in a glass of iced tea or potato salad.

Mullein Black (*Verbascum Nigrum*) (*Verbascum Thapsus*): Mullein tea is good for coughs and is used as an expectorant, decongestant, and mucous reducer. Making a salve of the leaves reduces skin inflammations, and the infused oil is used to treat earache.

Onion (*Allium Cepa*): Mars has dominion over the onion. The onion is not only good to eat, but it can also be beneficial in other ways. They were thought to be helpful against the bites of mad dogs and other venomous creatures when used with honey and rue; the seeds were said to increase sperm. The seeds kill worms in children if they drink the water in which the seeds have been soaking all night, after they have fasted and before breakfasting. The juice is good for scalds or burns, and combined with vinegar, it takes away skin blemishes.

Parsley (*Apium Petroselinum*): Parsley is probably the most-abused herb. Oftentimes, it is considered nothing more than a cheap garnish on a dinner plate, although it adds flavor to almost any dish. It is under Mercury and strengthens the stomach. The juice dropped into the ear eases an earache. Make a decoction of one cup of water and two ounces of the roots and tops reduced to a gill. Combine that with fennel, anise, including one ounce of their roots and one-half ounce of carraway seeds. Taken two or three times a day, it is good for jaundice, dropsy, and pain in the kidneys. Parsley has for years been a natural insect repellant. Farmers in Ireland plant a row of parsley around their potato fields for good luck, and the Chinese word for parsley means "kill flea."

Rosemary (*Rosemarinus Officinalis*): Rosemary is governed by the Sun in the celestial sign Aries. It is good for the memory and the digestive tracts, as well as treating nervous headaches and working as a breath freshener. It can be taken as a tea, summer or winter, by simply taking a cutting and brewing a tea.

Sage (*Salvia laterflora*): Sage is governed by Jupiter. It is good for mental derangements and nerves. It is good for the liver and blood and for the throat if used as a gargle. Make an infusion of three ounces of the dried leaves to one pint of boiling water, and take three tablespoons three or four times a day.

Strawberry (*Fragaria Vesca*): The strawberry plant is under Venus. It is a diuretic. The fresh leaves made into a tea is a good mouth wash for sore mouths and throat. For kidney and liver complaint, make a strong infusion of the leaves with a little ginger. Drink three or four eight-ounce glasses a day.

Tansy (*Tanacetum Vulgare*): Venus claims this herb. It is particularly suited for the diseases of women. It is good for the stomach, opens obstructions, promotes menses, and removes impurities by urination. It is rather stimulating. The crushed leaves relieve sprains, swellings, and fresh wounds. Make an infusion of powdered tansy, ½ drachm. Take one half cup two or three times a day.

Thyme (*Thymus Serpyllum*) (*Thymus Vulgaris*): Thyme is under Venus. An infusion of the leaves removes hangover-induced headaches. If taken before bed, it is said to ward off nightmares. The oil of thyme contains an antiseptic and is often added to cough syrups and gargles. For external use if thyme is made into a salve or ointment, it can help soothe sore muscles.

Violets (*Violoe Odorate Flores*): Violets are under the dominion of Venus. Fresh-gathered tops are used, the powder of which makes a good emetic. The flowers taken in one or two teaspoons will act as a laxative. For syrup of violets, take one pound of blooms along with three pints of boiling water, macerate overnight, pour off the liquid, and strain. By weight, add twice that of refined sugar and stir. Don't boil. One to two tablespoons will be a proper dosage. Violet leaves and flowers make a good salad.

Willow (*Salix*): Willow is governed by the moon. Take one ounce of willow bark and one pint of hot water and simmer for twenty or thirty minutes, adding at the end two teaspoons of cinnamon, then strain while hot. Take a six ounce glass two or three times a day, for intestinal disorders, dysentery, or intermittent fevers.

Additional Remedies
For Colds and Fever and Sore Throat:
Steep one-half teaspoon each of the dried leaves of summer savory, catnip, yarrow, and boneset in a cup of hot water. Stir, strain, and drink at once.

Gargle with apple cider vinegar every hour, one teaspoon of vinegar per glass of water. Drink or swallow the gargle when you are finished. In twelve to twenty-four hours, your sore throat will be gone.

To relieve a stuffy nose or nasal congestions, chew honeycomb three times a day.

For Poison Ivy:
Collect the leaves and stems of the jewel weed and sweet fern. This is best done in the fall. Hang them and dry until the leaves can be

crumbled easily (about a fortnight—two weeks) and crumble together. Store the herbs in a tightly-closed container. When needed, boil a large handful of the herbs in a quart of water for two minutes. Cool, strain, and apply the solution to the affected area every hour until relief comes.

Rub the leaves of a touch-me-not on the affected spot.

Make a mixture of vinegar and salt and put it on it. Or you can wet the affected area with water and put baking soda on the place.

Use equal parts of apple cider vinegar and water and dab on the affected area.

For Spider Bites:

Dissolve one heaping teaspoon of baking soda in a cup of cider vinegar. Soak a compress in the solution and apply directly to the bite. [Note: For black widow or brown recluse bites, go to the hospital emergency room or your doctor.]

For Bee Stings:

Take a wad of tobacco, wet it with warm water, and put it on the sting.

Make a paste of one teaspoon each of honey and baking soda and apply it to the sting.

Earache:

Blow smoke from rabbit tobacco in the ear. You can also use smoking tobacco, pipe, or cigarette.

Take the good meat out of a black walnut. Put it into a cloth, beat it, and dip it in warm water. Afterwards, squeeze the excess water and oil into the ear.

Put a few drops of olive oil (extra virgin--also known as sweet oil—works well) in the ear.

Put a drop or two of warm castor oil in the ear.

Fever:

Teas made from boneset, the roots of a butterfly weed, or horsemint are good for fevers and colds.

A tea made of rabbit tobacco will relieve a fever.

For Night Sweats:

If the skin surface is given a cupped-hand bath at bedtime, the night sweats will be prevented.

For Weight Loss:

Take one tablespoon of apple cider vinegar before each meal. The vinegar allows the body to use the fat it has stored and not to accumulate more. The patient does not give up any food normally eaten. This will allow about one inch to be lost in two months and ten pounds in a year.

A Safe Sedative:

Take one tablespoon of honey before going to bed. Mix three tablespoons of apple cider vinegar to one cup of honey. This will relieve nervous tension and allow you to sleep more soundly. Take two teaspoons within an hour of retiring, and it will quickly produce sleep.

An Old Fashioned Cough Remedy:

Boil one lemon for ten minutes. Cut the lemon in half, squeeze it, and put the juice in an ordinary glass. Add to the glass one ounce of glycerin, and then fill up the glass with honey. If you do not have a lemon, apple cider vinegar will work as a substitute. Take three times a day.

For Burns:

Apply honey to the burn. This produces rapid healing.

Apple cider vinegar, as it comes from the bottle, will take the soreness and smarting out of a burn. It is also good for relieving the pain of shingles.

For Tired, Red Eyes:

Boil one cup of water with one teaspoon of fennel seed. When the water turns golden, strain the seeds and allow the liquid to cool. Use as an eyewash.

A Good Liniment:

Beat up the yolk of one egg with one tablespoon of turpentine and one tablespoon of apple cider vinegar. Apply to the sore area.

For Sore Feet:

Apply castor oil to your feet and then sleep with white socks on. The next morning, your feet will be soft and the soreness gone.

To Shrink Varicose Veins:

Use apple cider vinegar on the veins at night, and they will shrink. Also, drink a glass of water twice a day with a tablespoon of apple cider vinegar added.

For Snakebite:

The only venomous snakes we are likely to encounter in Kentucky are pit vipers, copperheads, rattlesnakes, and water moccasins. They are hemotoxic, meaning they affect the blood and the venom is spread by the circulatory system. It is important to get the venom removed from the body or to get an antidote. Remember, if you are bitten, one-third of all bites are dry, without venom. Snakes eat about once a month, and if they have recently fed, then their venom reserve is low. Staying calm is important. The more excited you become, the faster the heart pumps the venom throughout the body. Only an average of three people a year die from snakebite, so the chances of death are very slim. A poultice of the burdock (cocklebur plant), using its boiled leaves directly on the wound, will help draw out the venom. My grandfather survived a copperhead bite as a child using this poultice, and he did not see a doctor. Tobacco, rabbit tobacco, baking soda, and other things have the ability to draw. Pieces of the heart and liver of an animal are also said to draw out poison.

Take the leaves of the burdock plant and boil them in water until a poultice can be made and applied to the bite. Change the poultice as the venom is drawn from the bite. Take the victim immediately to a doctor or hospital for an antidote.

Today, growing and using herbs and other natural material is an interesting and fun hobby. Years ago, it was a necessity. Doctors were few and far between, and there were many more types of injuries that could happen with open fires and sharp hand tools. People had to take care of themselves as best they could. I personally have been treated for earache, bee stings, burns, sunburns, colds, sore throats, and some other afflictions with remedies from this section. The fennel eyewash is especially good for me. Many of them I have never tried. Some of those have been used by other people I have known.

Most any housewife of the time knew of the commonly-used plants and had them growing in her yard. She knew what to do to prepare them. Leah Smock was taught this herbal art by her mother. They knew these old secrets as well as any in the area they lived. It was not only the Smocks that knew these things but also virtually everyone on the frontier. The knowledge of herbs came over with the colonists and was enhanced by the uses Native Americans had for these plants.

Conclusion, Tables, and Definitions

In concluding this chapter, it occurred to me that there are some terms and definitions that might need clarification. Indeed, some of them are not frequently in use today. For this reason, I have chosen a medical dictionary from 1940 to get most of the definitions. I did that for two reasons: firstly, it was a dictionary that was current when the remedies listed were more commonly in use, and secondly, the dictionary belonged to my mother who died in June 2010. As I looked up the definitions, I felt her smiling as I used her old textbook. My mother was a registered nurse and continued to use some of these remedies until very late in her life. I know she got a kick out of me using her textbook, anyway.

The measurements given are, as much as possible, converted to modern convention, but I will include a table with some equivalent weights and measures. Some of these remedies are taken from 16th century sources, and our modern weights and measures differ. Lastly, I want to recommend some books to the reader. The first book is a lot of fun and a good source of information, but it was written in the 17th century by William Joseph Semonite and Nicholas Culpepper. It is entitled *The Semonite-Culpepper Herbal Remedies: The Medicinal Property of Herbs and Directions for Compounding the Prescriptions of Curative Medicines*. The next two books are excellent sources for the gardener and herbalist and those seeking to make home remedies. The first is entitled *Grow Your Own Drugs*, by James Wong. In it, there are more than sixty recipes for home remedies. This book has excellent color plates of many of the seeds, roots, and plants described. The second of these books is *The Complete Guide to Herbal Medicines*, by Charles W. Fetrow, Pharm. D. and Juan R. Avila, Pharm. D. In this 698 page book, there are over seventy contributors, including doctors, pharmacists, and others in the medical profession. Both of these books are excellent resources. I recommend them.

Definitions

Aperient: 1. Mildly cathartic. 2. A gentle purgative.[56]

Decoction: 1. The process of boiling. 2. A preparation made by boiling.[57]

Diuretic: A medicine that promotes the flow of urine.[58]

Dropsy: The accumulation of serous fluid in a cavity or in the tissues.[59]

Emetic: A medicine that causes vomiting.[60]

Expectorant: A medicine that aids expectoration (the coughing up of sputum from the air passages).[61]

Fomentation: A warm application, usually moist.[62]

Gout: A painful constitutional disease with joint inflammation and chalky deposits.[63]

Infusion: The steeping of a substance in water for obtaining its soluble principles; also the solution so obtained.[64]

Lepra: Same as leprosy, also psoriasis.[65]

Macerate: To cause to become soft or separated into constituent elements by, or as if, by steeping fluid; *broadly*: steep, soak ~ vi: to soften and wear away, from being wetted or steeped.[66]

Rheumatism: A constitutional disease marked by pain in the joints or muscles, usually recurrent, and often due to exposure.[67]

Scurvy: A disease due to deficiency of vitamin C, marked by weakness, anemia, spongy gums, and mucocutaneous (pertaining to mucous membranes) hemorrhages.[68]

Table of Weights and Measures[69]

A Pound = 12 ounces*

A pound of liquid = 4 gills

An ounce = 8 drachms

A drachm (liquid) = 3 scruples

A dram (solid) = 1/16th ounce

A scruple = 20 grains

A gallon = 8 pints

A pint = 16 ounces

A tablespoon of fluid = ½ ounce

A fluid ounce = 8 fluid drachms

*A pound today is considered 16 ounces. The 12 ounce figure is from a 17th century source, Semonite and Culpepper.

Dosage, or, the Art of Prescribing Medicine

Generally, unless otherwise specified in the remedies, Semmonite and Culpepper states, "For an adult, suppose the dose to be I drachm"—

Under one year will require only 1/12 (or 5 grains)

Under two years will require only 1/8 (or 8 grains)

Under three years will require only 1/6 (or 10 grains)

Under four years will require only 1/4 (or 15 grains)

Under seven years will require only 1/3 (or 1 scruple)

Under fourteen years will require only 1/2 (or 1/2 drachm)

Under twenty years will require only 2/3 (or 2 scruples)

Above twenty-one years the full dose 1 (or 1 drachm)

Above sixty-five, the inverse graduation of the above.[70]

Chapter 9

ECONOMICS AND RELIGIOUS EXPANSION

A Synopsis

If we have learned anything about the meaning of witchcraft in Western Europe, it is that it may have evolved for the last 30,000 years until the 14th century from a fertility cult that was pre-Christian. It changed over time as the societies in which it once flourished grew in population and expanded their economies. The hunting-gathering bands that moved about following the seasonal changes of their environment began to bury their dead in a careful reverent way and created images of their chief gods and goddesses. They had a pantheon of gods that were represented in the flora, fauna, natural objects, and climatic conditions provided by their environment, and over time, their religion evolved from animism to polytheism. That shift was a natural evolution in religious thought that changed as their society and economy grew more complex. The reduction in the number of gods to two, a god and a goddess, provided their worshipers with a simpler way to control the uncontrollable. This reduction in gods may have given rise to the notion of clan totems. The animistic gods were reshaped and perpetuated, albeit in a different and less important but still respectable way, as a bear or perhaps wolf clan. The old animistic gods were not forgotten but were assigned new positions in the culture.

From perhaps as far back as 500,000 years, man learned from his environment what plants were good to eat and what plants held curative properties. He learned the seasonal changes and the pattern of stars and the frequency of their appearance. And man knew what those things meant. The stars and position of the sun told them when to move from the summer or fall camp to the winter one higher in the elevations. It determined the mating seasons of the mega fauna that inhabited their range and when the hunting was most favorable. Although these people were Stone Age hunters and gatherers, they were not the crude, unsophisticated cavemen of the comic books. Their culture was less complex, but it served them as well as ours today serves us. Sympathetic magic was a way to sort of help the gods help them. They modeled animals in clay and pierced their vitals with spears and arrows as they intended to do the following day. They devised ceremonies, deep within the caves, to initiate young men into the tribe and to ensure success in the hunt. There was no room for those that did not produce. A division of labor was decided along gender lines. Women did the work that had to be done and could be done while rearing and nursing children. The men did the things that could not be done with children, such as hunting, defense, and the like. Later, when the planting of grain and the domestication of animals expanded their economy and allowed more free time, specialists developed. Before food surpluses (farming) came into being, there was no room for a priestly class, artists, or specialized workers.

Animal husbandry and agriculture led to a surplus of food, and in the Iron Age, that meant wealth. Wealth was having excess produce that could be sold or traded for goods not readily available, which also meant that wealth made its possessors a target for those who did not have the means or ability to produce it themselves. Thus, for self-protection, family groups or clans settled together. This grouping of peoples led to clusters of residences to organize into hamlets, towns, and cities. Throughout this time, the polytheistic pagan religions persisted and grew, probably seeing their greatest advancement in the 4th and 5th century Druids. Even though the Druids were put down by the force of Rome, the old gods continued to be worshipped unmolested, until the 14th century Inquisition, where millions of people were burned as heretics or witches. Most of these were healers, herbalists, astrologers, and midwives. They carried on the traditions, some of which began in the caves of France thirty millennia ago. As a matter of self-preservation, these folks were forced to adopt Catholicism and then later to convert to various other forms of Christian faith. They became Christian but kept some of the traditions alive. The church actually aided this process when they adopted some of the pagan festivals and gave them Christian meaning.

The people that continued these traditions worked in secret, and some made their way to the colonies in America. The colonies were rife with the belief in the Devil. The painted heathen savages were considered the Devil incarnate. The woods were dark and fearsome. No wonder the climate was right for the witch hysteria that enveloped Salem. By 1700, the witchcraft scares were over but the fear of the Devil still existed. In the early 1700s, the first school law passed in New England was "The Deluder Satan Act." This act reinforced the concept of demonic possession by an anthropomorphic devil. The act stated that, from time to time, the Devil walking about on the Earth would possess a student, and it was the teacher's duty to "beat the Devil out of the child." The effects of this law, corporal punishment, is still with us today, and it stems from the belief in witches and their leader the Devil.

Kentucky

The nature of mankind forces men people to find what lies beyond the next hill and valley and keeps them moving always further. The English looked to the colonies, dreaming of free or cheap land and the lure of riches in furs, salt, precious metals, and a fresh beginning. These desires were the driving force for immigration to the colonies and thence westward. In the colonies, land could often be had for the taking.

The colonies had been populated, and although linked together under the English Crown, they were divided into regions (northern, middle and southern) not only by geography but also by their economies. Each region had a different environmental and economic set of needs. The southern colonies, with their milder climate, longer growing seasons, and richer soil, developed an agrarian economy augmented with shipping and fishing in the coastal communities. Because there were no modern means of farming, all farm implements were either used by hand or were horse-drawn, and slave labor was perhaps the only effective way to do large-scale plantation (single crop) farming. In the middle colonies, fishing, whaling, shipping, import, export mercantile, and later manufacturing were the mainstays of the economy, with less emphasis on farming. In the northern colonies, timber, furs, fishing, and farming anchored that economy.

The upshot of these regional differences is that the colonies interacted and depended on one another. The southern colonies exported produce and cotton and traded with the middle colonies for manufactured goods, whale oil, and imported English products. The middle colonies needed the English imports but also the farm produce and cotton to make cloth. They also needed the timber from the northern colonies to build ships and to export timber, specifically long pine ship masts to England and other European countries. The land was poorer and the growing season was shorter in the northern colonies, so they traded with the middle colonies for southern produce and cotton or finished cotton goods. A constant demand for all of the needed goods perpetuated this economic interaction. The result was a further migration westward, as the animals and timber from the Eastern forests were depleted. Crop rotation was unknown, developing a need for new crop land. Westward migration became a necessity.

In Western Europe, church persecution of another sort was a direct result of the Reformation, education, and the printing press. More people could now read and interpret the Bible for themselves. The Bible was being printed in English, German, and other languages. This freedom of thought and ability to read and determine in each man's mind what the Bible meant led to disagreements within the Anglican Church (Church of England). The Puritans, Baptist Dunkards, John Wesley and his Methodists, and others formed their own ideas and attracted followers, and their ideas were unwelcome in England. These people, many of whom were looked down upon in the old country, found a new start in the colonies. The freedom of being able to read and interpret the scriptures for themselves led to modifications of existing ideas and expanded Protestant denominations. The colonies and the frontier of Kentucky were ripe for religious freedom, and Protestant and Catholic pioneers brought religion to the Bluegrass state. This didn't just happen–explorers and long hunters paved the way by cutting roads, building forts or stations, and guiding parties through the Cumberland Gap into the wilds of Kentucky.

One of the frontier explorers who opened the door to Kentucky with his explorations and Indian encounters is forever linked to Kentucky. Daniel Boone along with his younger brother, Squire, explored the area of Kentucky where the Leah Smock incident actually took place.

The Boones were Quakers from Devonshire, England, and lived as farmers and weavers. They had broken away from the Anglican Church and been punished with fines, ostracism, prison, and whippings. They could not hold office, attend schools, or vote. They could not train for scholarly professions. In other words, they were true second-class citizens. The Boones had been settled in Devonshire around the city of Exeter for more than two hundred years. The region had been under the influence or rule of the Romans, Saxons, Normans, and Tudors. Many Quakers had already gone to the New World in the 1600s. William Penn, the son of an admiral highly respected by King Charles II, had been inspired by the Inner Light as a youth and was expelled from Oxford University for refusing to attend Anglican services. By 1678, there were hundreds of Quakers from Yorkshire living in New Jersey. Some had crossed the Delaware into what would become Pennsylvania.[71]

Squire Boone, who would later become the father of Daniel Boone, married Sarah Morgan soon after he arrived in America. The Morgans were from a part of Wales that was mountainous and known for its crags and tors. The Welsh had always loved a religion of praise and independence, preferring to seek peace, liberty, and happiness on their own terms and in their own rugged world.[72] Is it any wonder Daniel explored?

Immigrants to America came here to settle in a place where their religious thoughts did not cause persecution. The 1730s and 1740s were a time of religious revival in the American colonies, when the movement called the Great Awakening was sweeping over the land. But it was also a time when parents and churches seemed to be losing control over their young. More and more young women had children out of wedlock. There is a tradition in American humor and folklore that religious revivals also inspire a surge in illegitimate births, as religious fervor seems to stir sexual fever. Such revivals, it was said, "led to more souls being made than saved." After the great revival at Cane Ridge, Kentucky, in 1801, it was reported, "Becca Bell 'is with child to one Brown', Kate Cummins also 'got careless' and 'had a bastard'; Patty McGuire has been whoring.'" The reverend Charles Woodsmason, who traveled into the Carolina backcountry at this time, noted that ninety-four percent of the brides whom he married in the last year were pregnant on their wedding days.[73] This sounds more like the results of the festivals of the Old Religion than the puritanical teachings of the new. Perhaps wilder places and times encourage deeply-buried passions within the psyche of men and women to manifest; if so, then the wilderness of Kentucky certainly provided an enticing environment for that to happen.

The first permanent settlement in Kentucky was at old Fort Harrod, erected in 1774 and 1775 in what is now called Harrodsburg, Kentucky. There were no women or children accompanying the original thirty-two men. Three families did arrive before the completion of the fort. Numerous families arrived in 1775 and 1776.[74] William and Morgan Bryant, brothers of Rebecca Bryant Boone, Daniel's wife, built a hunting camp of several cabins at what became Bryant's Station, near Lexington, Kentucky, in 1774. By 1782, it became the largest fort in Kentucky. In 1775, Boonesborough was established by Daniel Boone and a company of men on a rise above the banks of the Kentucky River. From these places, Daniel and his brother, Squire, as well as many other hunters and pioneer explorers, began to push further west to explore this area of what was then part of Virginia.

Meade County, Kentucky

Meade County, Kentucky, was a virtual wilderness in 1775. It was a hunter's paradise filled with wild game of all kinds. A karst region with underlying limestone deposits of the Ordovician Period that provided a pioneer industry was maintained until the last half of the 19th century, the "lime kiln industry." The knobs and hills are as high as six hundred feet above sea level and have little flat ground on their summits. Springs and caves abound throughout the county. Between the seams of limestone, chert deposits exist, from which the Native Americans fashioned their stone spear and arrow points. Glacial till in the form of smooth river cobbles provided the material for them to fashion stone axes. The Ohio River is the northwest boundary between the county and the state of Indiana. Hardin and Breckenridge counties border to the south and east, the river to the north and west. Meade County has the largest Ohio River boundary of any county in the Commonwealth of Kentucky, with fifty-six miles of river frontage. The river made Meade County an important point for riverboat ports, such as Brandenburg, Richardson's Landing, Moorman Landing, and others.

Bear, deer, rabbits, squirrels, passenger pigeons, ducks, geese, quail, doves, and wild turkey provided meat for the earliest settlers. Bear, wolves, panthers, and bobcats provided some danger to livestock and, occasionally, people. Nut meats from the hazel bushes and hickory, walnut, chestnut, and beech trees, as well as wild strawberry, blackberry, raspberry, huckleberry, and elderberry bushes provided sustenance throughout the seasons. Before the white men came to Kentucky, the territory in the great bend of the Ohio River from the mouth of Otter Creek to the mouth of Sinking Creek was a veritable hunters' paradise.[75]

In 1780, Daniel Boone built a hunting camp and planted a patch of ground at the "Boone Spring" near Big Spring, Kentucky. The following year, he returned with Edward Bulger. They remained at the camp and planted a patch of land.[76] Squire and Daniel made several trips to the area, and Squire, a Baptist minister, preached throughout Meade County in "brush arbor" meetings, from Otter Creek to Wolf Creek, to Paradise Bottoms to Cedar Flat to the area that would become Staples, later to be changed, in 1885, to Battletown, Kentucky.[77] On June 18, 1781, eighteen converted Baptists met under a large sugar maple tree and founded the first Baptist Church in Meade County at Wolf Creek. In those days, Indian attacks on the settlements occurred with frequency, and attending a church meeting could be hazardous. Lookouts armed with Kentucky long rifles had to be on watch to ensure the safety of the members. Huron (locally called Wyandotte), Shawnee, Cherokee, Mingo and Delaware Indians were always looking for an opportunity to drive out the white settlers. Squire held open-air meetings near Blue Spring and Doe Run. In 1815, Wolf Creek Baptist Church was the first of four established churches in this area. Church services in those days were far different from services today. People rode on horseback or in wagons to services that were held once a month, regardless of the weather. Meetings might be held in the open air or in the houses and barns of the congregation. The congregation knelt during the service while one deacon sang his prayers, and other deacons sometimes cried as he prayed. Services were hours long, and baptisms were held at nearby ponds, even in winter when ice had to be broken to submerge the person being baptized. I suspect many people prayed for their conversions to take place during warmer weather.

In those days, you would not hear a Baptist preacher use the words "altar," "pulpit," "pew," "church house," "sacrament," or recite the Apostle's Creed, for those were an offense. The preacher mounted a stand, preached to the congregation seated on benches, administered the ordinances, read the scriptures, and lined out the hymns. Lining out hymns was a practice where the preacher sang the first line, followed by the congregation repeating the line. This system was used in early churches because hymn books were costly and many people could not read. The congregation assembled at a meeting house or a meeting place. Every church circulated subscriptions (offerings) to compensate the ministry. Every member was expected to make a subscription.[78] Such was the early state of religion in old Meade County.

Squire Boone lost all of his money and lands in Kentucky, and the man who conducted the first white marriage in Kentucky was penniless. Squire Boone's family persuaded the fifty-seven-year-old to return with them to Kentucky from Missouri, where he had been on another exploration with brother, Daniel. He returned to find that his land holdings had evaporated, back taxes were due, and unscrupulous land attorneys, known as "land sharks," had taken title to his properties. On May 18, 1804, a few days after his return, the proud defender of the wilderness, this noble, scrupulously honest, Christian pioneer, was thrown into prison in Louisville for non-payment of debt. But he was soon released by friends who came to his rescue and paid his outstanding debts. He determined to leave Kentucky forever, and he did.[79] Daniel had preceded him in leaving Kentucky and resided in Missouri. Squire moved across the river from Meade County and took up residence near a cave that had hid him from attacking Indians. He built a mill there and founded Goshen Baptist Church, where he preached, and because the cave saved his life, he considered this area of Indiana holy ground.

Part 2

The Legend of Leah Smock and Discussion of Contemporary 19th Century American Witchcraft

Chapter 10
WITCHCRAFT IN PIONEER KENTUCKY AND TENNESSEE

Native American Beliefs and Occult Practices

It is my belief that whatever practices from the remnants of the European Old Religion that immigrated to America were influenced by two cultures, Native American and West African, the latter brought to this continent directly by the slave trade and indirectly by the Haitian slave revolt. At the time of white contact, there were many American Indian beliefs, myths, legends, and occult practices, all active parts of the Native American culture. Indian Joe, the Native American friend of Leah Smock, would have been familiar with many of them. He likely shared these superstitions, as well as healing herbal lore, with Leah. I have selected two Indian cultures (the Cherokee and the Delaware) that made war in Kentucky and within ten years of the Leah Smock incident were, for the most part, removed west of the Mississippi River. The Seminole Nation, a third contemporary culture at the same time existing in Florida, Georgia, and Alabama. West of the Mississippi River, I chose the Washoe Indians of the northwest and the Apache of the southwest, covering that region of the United States north to south. While this is a representative sample of cultural beliefs, it will be seen that similarities exist between all of these cultures.

This chapter also covers additional 19th century witchcraft incidents occurring in Kentucky, Tennessee, and Louisiana, approximately one hundred years after the Salem witch crisis. There may well be connections, no matter how slight, between the case of Marie Laveau, the Salem witches, and Tituba. The purpose of this chapter is to provide an understanding of what Indian Joe might have shared with Leah. It also discusses historical witchcraft events known in Appalachia and other areas of Kentucky.

Delaware Native American Practices

Kentuckians and Tennesseans were occasionally fighting Indians up until President Andrew Jackson's Indian Removal Act of May 28 1830. This act was designed to move the Indians residing east of the Mississippi River to areas reserved for them west of the river. The war of 1812 ended some fifteen years earlier, and the Indian lands of the Cherokee, Chickasaw, and Seminole were coveted by the Jackson administrations' supporters, and although the Supreme Court upheld the Indian claims, these Native American people were displaced by the army and their lands confiscated. This displacement resulted in the Trail of Tears, a forced march in which many Native Americans died along the way west.

That the Indians existed alongside the pioneers for years allowed interactions between them to take place. This interaction continued, as evidenced by Leah Smock's association with the mysterious figure, Indian Joe. Leah and Joe's relationship began sometime between 1834 and 1838 and continued until her death in 1840. He was likely a Huron, locally known as Wyandotte or Guyandotte, living in Indiana opposite Lapland. Whether Leah and Joe met in Indiana and he followed the Smocks to Kentucky or whether he was from Indiana at all is speculation. He lived for a long time near Battletown, Kentucky, perhaps eighty-five years or more. He became a friend and likely confidant of Leah. It has been speculated that he shared his knowledge of Native American lore and sorcery with Leah, a proposition believed by many.

Native Americans had knowledge of herbs, myths and legends, witchcraft, sorcery and a belief in ghosts. In addition, the tribes contained a group of powerful men and women known variously as shaman, sachem, medicine men, or healers. Depending on the culture, the shaman could be male or female. Anyone who had power had the potential to be a shaman, and all shamans had the potential to become a sorcerer or witch. Even in Indian cultures, the potential to do good or evil existed in everyone, regardless of gender. All Native American nations have similar but varying beliefs extending north and south and from coast to coast.

The Delaware were an East Coast nation that gradually moved westward due to white incursions into their land. The Delaware were often known as Lenape and originally occupied the mid-Atlantic area of New Jersey, northern Delaware, eastern Pennsylvania, and southern New York.[80] They were an Algonquin people and were among the first Indians to welcome European Settlers 450 years ago. They aligned themselves with the Iroquois, Shawnee, Mingo, and Cherokee to fight the later incursions of white settlers into their lands. The Lenape were pushed further and further to the west and at times lived in Indiana and Ohio before moving west to Missouri, Arkansas, Texas, Kansas, and Oklahoma. Some migrated to Wisconsin and Ontario, Canada. On their western migration, they joined with the Shawnee, Mingo, Cherokee, Chickasaw, and others to fight and hunt in the no man's land of Kentucky. At the time of discovery and settlement, Kentucky was a huge communal hunting preserve for all of the tribes and nations. Very few Indian villages were erected in historic Kentucky and only one or two of any permanency.

The Delaware used spells, believed in witches, and knew the use of herbs for medicine. They believed in spirits, ghosts, monsters, and giants. There is an entity known as WAY-MAH-TAH-KUN-EESE or Little Warrior. This entity is a messenger from the Great Spirit and is always dressed in war gear. He is a spirit about the size of a child. He appears to warriors and hunters in times of war and protects them in battle and visits them when they are alone. He commissions some braves with supernatural powers that cause them to influence other people and make them do things against their will. These people so endowed cannot be harmed or killed in battle.[81] While this messenger seems to have a specialized task, he is reminiscent of the medieval European witch familiar that does the witches bidding and delivers messages in times of need.

There are two similar legends that relate the belief in a magical talisman handed down generationally by the Delaware. The two legends are that of the Great Bear and the Great Naked Bear. The Great Bear was supposed to be the king of all the bears. He was a very ferocious bear and fast traveler. He was a constant terror to hunters, and his visage was used to frighten children when they were disobedient. This Great Bear was wounded in battle with a mastodon, and the Great Spirit appeared to a brave and told him that if he would secure the mastodon's tusk from the bear, it would act as magic in case of sickness or injury. The hunter followed the bear and found it asleep on a cliff. It was several times larger than a regular bear, and the hunter knew he could not kill it. The Great Spirit told the hunter that the tusk was broken during the fight, and if the hunter would creep up on the bear while it was sleeping, he could pull out the tusk. The hunter did, but the bear awoke and the hunter had to jump. A cedar tree broke his fall, and he got away. The tusk has been kept for years, and the Delaware have great faith in its magic.

There is a similar story told by the Delaware and the Mohicans. There was a huge beast of a bear, immense in size and ferocity. Its skin was bare except for a tuft of white hair on its back. It ate Indians, and the only means of escape from it was by water. Its heart was very small, making it hard to kill. The last one known was in the east beyond the left bank of the Mahicanni Siper, the Hudson River. *Note: In Shawnee sipi means river. In Delaware Siper means river. The Mississippi River's third syllable is sippi or river.* When the warriors hunted the last naked bear, they climbed a tall rock and made a noise to attract the bear and then shot it with arrows and threw great stones at him and, thus, killed him. Indian mothers would frighten their children into obedience, threatening them with the words: "The Naked Bear will eat you."[82]

The Delaware, Iroquois, and Shawnee called their shaman "sachem." Once there was a young man who was endowed with power by a water manitou, this spirit gave him the ability to play the flute. When he was a small boy, he learned the lessons of the medicine men.

All are possessed of certain influences, although we may not know it. When they know the way we got the power, all we have to do is be firm and brave to succeed. If we fail it's not because our guardian spirit is not faithful because we listen to the voices of others and not to our spirit that would give success.

When he was a man, he had great success as a hunter and was considered to be a conjuror or medicine man, and the people were drawn to him by some unknown power. The old medicine men became angry because of his success, and they began to contrive some way to get rid of him by conjury.

The young man told his mother that the medicine men were trying to kill him, and if they did, she should tie his flute to his wrist and throw his body in the water without ceremony. While the medicine men were trying to figure out how to kill the young man, an old woman who lived alone and was believed to be a witch said she could kill him, so they agreed to let her try. The young man knew the water manitou had greater power than the evil manitou that guarded the witch. The young man told his mother that the witch would succeed in killing him. And she did.

The evil medicine men came to the mother and offered to give the young man an elaborate funeral and dress him in finery, but she said no. She told them that she believed him to be killed and that his body should be treated as such and simply thrown away. She tied his flute to his wrist and threw him in the river. Six days later, she heard him playing his flute. The young man lived with the Delaware for years and had many friends, but the sachem and the witch soon died because they could not forget the way they killed him.[83]

Cherokee Native American Practices

The Cherokee had similar myths and legends. They believed there were seven cardinal directions: north, south, east and west, above, below, and in between. There were also seven heavens. There was a white spirit of peace and a black specter of death. Most things in nature were believed to have spirits, rocks, trees, animals, caves, and such. Ghosts and spirits of the dead hovered around their former homes. The chief held a ceremony in honor of the first new moon of spring in early March. Days later, when the chief set the date, the Friendship Dance was held. On the second morning, the chief acting as the high priest brought out a sacred crystal that was believed to foretell the future. It was of the purest quartz. The crystal predicted the success of the crops.[84]

The Cherokee Raven Mocker was an evil witch who could be male or female but more often was female. Raven Mocker, ka'lanu ahkyeli'ski, steals the life left to men and women, usually old ones, by magically removing their hearts and leaving no scar. With no evidence to the contrary, the death is considered natural. These witches appear as old men and women because they add to their lives whatever years their victims had left to live. Thus, they are very old.

When someone in the village is dying, the Raven Mocker flies through the air in a fiery shape, making a call like a raven. When the Raven Mocker gets to the house of the person who is ill, he or she will usually find other Raven Mockers there waiting. They become invisible and go inside the house to torment and kill the victim. They sometimes lift the victim and throw them on the floor, slitting their head or scalp. Friends and relatives think it is the patient having convulsions or trying to breathe and falling by his or her own actions. Only a few medicine men can recognize the Raven Mockers, and when the elderly get sick, their relatives often hire a medicine man to stand guard against the Raven Mocker.[85] Burning is one way to kill a Raven Mocker. Interestingly, there is a parallel to the Cherokee Raven Mocker legend in British Columbia in Canada. The Kwakwak'waka have a secret society named Hamatsa, which is or was a cannibal society. In the Hamatsa dance, a raven mask with three beaks is said to be utilized to slit open the skull, so the ravens can more easily feed on the brain. The mask is a frightening image of the bird. Part of the Hamatsa lore contains legends of man-eating birds of prey.[86]

Seminole Native American Practices

In Florida, the Seminole Indians also have some similar beliefs. The Seminole believe in a Great Spirit. Some consider him beneficent, while others see him as impersonal. There are also lesser spirits, some good and some bad. They can be likened to angels and demons and can be propitiated by offerings or suitable prayers. Some of the spirits live in the sky world, while others live in a subterranean world. All living things and inanimate objects, including man-made ones, have spirits. These spirits are released when the person who owns them dies and friends and relatives break the objects The souls of people eventually make their way to the spirit world but not until they remain on the earth as ghosts. When a death takes place, it is best to abandon the village and move. The sun, moon, rainbow, and other such manifestations of nature are supernatural and are either spirits or the work of spirits. The Seminole believe in the existence of a number of creatures. These include mischievous little man-like dwarfs that live in the ground and giant serpents that roam the swamps or live in charms and talismans.[87]

The white man may scoff at the Seminole because the former doesn't believe in little dwarfs, but his great-great-great grandmother did and sat out bowls of milk for them. He will not plant crops, geld stock, or kill hogs unless the moon is right. He goes to an old man who, in his wisdom, tells him when to do these things. He also believes the souls make a journey to the afterworld but linger on earth as ghosts, and nothing can convince him to sleep in a cemetery overnight. He attaches supernatural meaning to natural occurrences, such as ball lightning and will-o-the-wisps. He puts faith in talismans, such as a rabbit's foot

Artist's conception of a figure from the Cave Les Trois Freres, depicting a man dancing upright wearing the head and hide of a bison. He appears to be playing a musical instrument of some kind, and is shown with a herd of bison. This figure may be a shaman or a portrayal of a god ensuring success in the hunt. This image is believed to have been made 15,000 years B.P. (before present).

An artist's conception of the controversial Wizard of Les Trois Freres. It shows a man dressed in the hide and wearing the horns of an elk or deer. It is believed that this figure sometimes called the Sorcerer dates from 15,000 B.P. and is supposed to be a mystical spirit, being, or god of the animals. The chamber in which it was found is called the Sanctuary, and from the illustrations depicted there it was used in magical rites.

Artist's conception of a drawing from the cave Les Trois Freres showing a bison depicted with spears and arrows piercing or pointing out vital organs. It is believed to be an example of sympathetic magic similar to piercing an object in order to inflict pain or death on a subject from afar, but it could also be an example made to teach young hunters the location of vital organs of the bison prior to the hunt. 15,000 years B.P.

The goat-footed horned figure of Pan, or Fauns from the Greco/Roman era may have been a continuation and evolution of the earlier figures found in the caves. Author's collection.

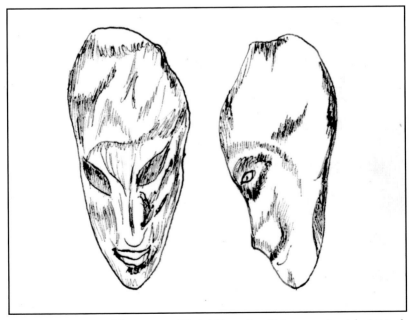

Artist's conception of the Venus of Dolni Vestonice. This approximately 1.5 inch ivory carving was found near Moravia in the Czech Republic during excavations in 1924. It dates to about 26,000 B.P. It is believed to be of a female figure, and may have indicated a personage of high rank. It is possible that these female figurines may have represented goddesses. Author's collection.

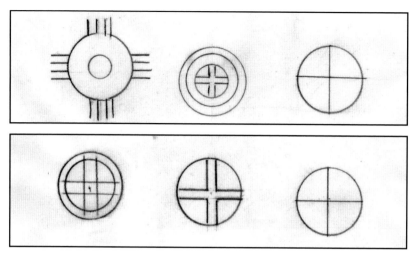

An example of the multilinear evolution of ideas. The top row contains examples of Eastern Hemisphere Assyrian designs, compared with Western Hemisphere Native American designs in the bottom row. Ideas can develop independently across the earth in cultures widely separated by geographic barriers like oceans and mountain ranges. Many times these ideas, which can include dress, ceramics, architecture, or tools, come about by similar environments, where cultures independently satisfy those cultural needs in a similar manner.

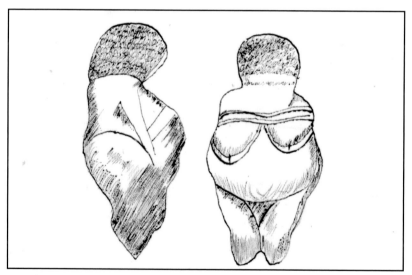

Artist's conception of the Venus of Willendorf. This figure was sculpted of limestone between 28,000 and 25,000 years B.P. It was found in Austria near the town of Krems. The models of women depicted in Late Paleolithic times usually have exaggerated breasts and genitalia. Early peoples were concerned with the animals they hunted and the propagation of the band, thus procreation and hunting dominated their art. This statue may be a depiction of a real woman, or that of a deity.

Artist's conceptions of horned figures in Europe and America. Top is the Green Man of the Woods, from Britain. It is a foliate mask showing a horned god of nature with leaves for the hair and beard. Foliate masks were carved into church doors, pews, and furniture by the craftsmen who depicted the old gods in the new Christian Churches. Examples of these figures can be found in the medieval exhibit of the castle room at the Speed Art Museum in Louisville, Kentucky. Center is a Native American wooden mask showing a man with the antlers of a deer. Whether this is a god image is not clear, but the horns and antlers denoted power and masculinity, and the rendering is of a mask found on Marco Island in Florida. Bottom is the artist rendering of the old western European god Cernunnos, a Celtic hunter god of beasts. He wears the forked antlers of a deer with warrior torcs decorating the antlers. Torcs were considered symbols of warrior rank from eight or nine hundred B.C. until about 300 A.D., after falling out of use they were readopted in Viking times.

The war chief Geronimo was well known for being clairvoyant and to possess great power as a healer. He had a premonition or revelation that his base camp had been attacked while he was with a small raiding party 125 miles distant. As might be expected his healing expertise was in healing battle wounds. This photograph was taken while he was still at war with the U.S. Army. Author's collection.

Statue of Squire Boone in front of his reconstructed church at Goshen, Indiana just north of Laconia. Squire was a Baptist minister that preached in the Lapland Staples area in pioneer Kentucky. The meetings were often brush arbor affairs held out of doors. Squire settled about a mile from this church where he found refuge and a hiding place in a cave when being heavily pursued by Indians. He left Kentucky and built a mill near the cave and prospered. He founded the Goshen Church, and when the monthly meetings were held, the congregation would become nervous as Wyandotte Indians would press their faces to the glass windows to watch the men and women worship and sing. Author's collection.

John Smock's grave in the Cunningham Cemetery. He and his daughter Elizabeth are buried near each other. John was born May 16, 1797 and died February 11, 1876. John was Leah's father. Photo courtesy of Shirley Brown.

Margaret and John Smock, the parents of Leah Smock. John was from New Jersey and Margaret from Pennsylvania, not far from where Homan wrote and published his Pow Wow book of charms and spells, "The Long Lost Friend." They married in Washington County, Virginia and lived there nine years, likely moving to Marion County, Kentucky, thence to Indiana and finally to the area of Battletown, Kentucky. Margaret was said to be a powerful Kentucky witch and taught her craft to Leah. Photo courtesy of Shirley Brown.

Blanford Ballard and Elizabeth Smock. Elizabeth was a child when Leah was killed. There are no known photographs of Leah, but some idea of her size and looks can be estimated by looking at Elizabeth, and Elizabeth's daughter Arigusta Singleton. Leah was said to be a beautiful girl with long dark hair. Photo courtesy of Shirley Brown.

The grave of Elizabeth Smock in the Cunningham Cemetery. David Ellis, son of Shirley Brown, in the background overlooks Elizabeth's toppled tombstone. Vines and brambles had to be cut and pulled to uncover the grave. Photo courtesy of Shirley Brown.

An overview of Leah's grave in the Betsy Daily Cemetery. Trees have fallen across her grave and little care has been given the cemetery that ceased being used in the 1920's. Photo courtesy of Shirley Brown.

A close up of Leah Smock's grave, showing the remnants of stones that were carried there by neighbors who dug down into her grave and filled it with field stones in order to keep Leah in the grave. A passerby saw Leah hovering above her grave in a long white dress. She was surrounded in a purple haze. Her form stopped short of the ground, and she was staring at the place she was buried. Photo courtesy of Shirley Brown.

Young Arigusta: Arigusta was the child of Elizabeth Smock and Blandford Ballard. She was a beautiful child said to closely resemble Leah. From her photograph we can get some idea of how Leah looked.

Family photograph of John and Arigusta Singleton. Back row, left to right: Bertha Singleton and Ethel Singleton, future grandmother of Shirley Brown. Front row, left to right: Lawrence Singleton, John Singleton holding Otis Singleton, and Arigusta Singleton holding Beckham Singleton and Marshall Singleton. Marshall is wearing a dress as is Otis. In those days it was customary for boys to wear a dress until the age of five or six years. Photo courtesy of Shirley Brown.

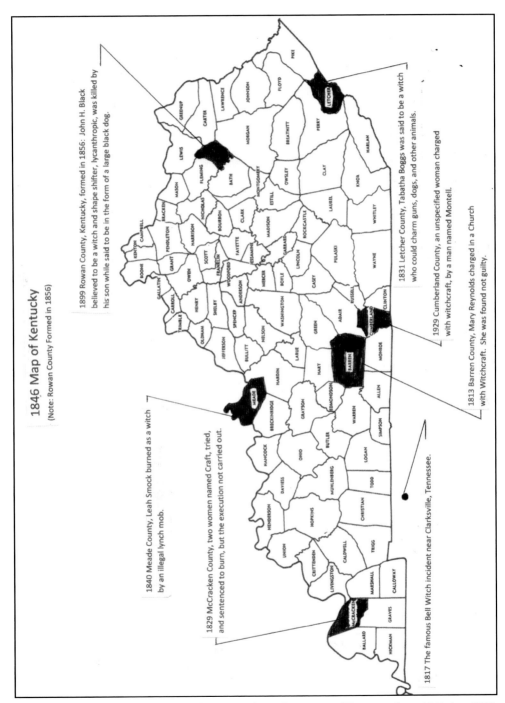

1846 Map of Kentucky
(Note: Rowan County Formed in 1856)

1899 Rowan County, Kentucky, formed in 1856: John H. Black believed to be a witch and shape shifter, lycanthropic, was killed by his son while said to be in the form of a large black dog.

1831 Letcher County, Tabatha Boggs was said to be a witch who could charm guns, dogs, and other animals.

1929 Cumberland County, an unspecified woman charged with witchcraft, by a man named Montell.

1813 Barren County, Mary Reynolds charged in a Church with Witchcraft. She was found not guilty.

1840 Meade County, Leah Smock burned as a witch by an illegal lynch mob.

1829 McCracken County, two women named Craft, tried, and sentenced to burn, but the execution not carried out.

1817 The famous Bell Witch incident near Clarksville, Tennessee.

Map of recorded incidents of witchcraft in Kentucky and environs of Tennessee from 1813 thru 1929.

Shirley Brown, great-great-great niece of Leah Smock

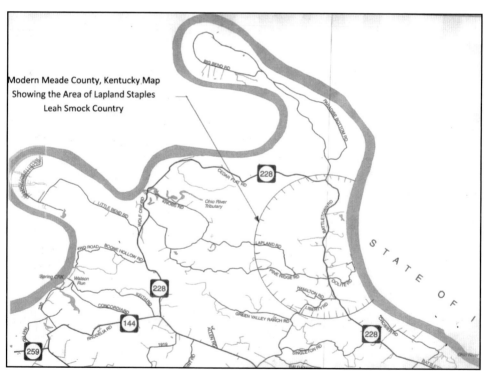

A Modern Map of the Lapland Staples Area of Meade County, Kentucky.

Gerald Fischer (left) with Leah's great-great niece, Shirley Brown, at Leah's gravesite. Photo courtesy of Kay Hamilton.

Kay Hamilton and husband Joe Mack Hamilton. Author's collection.

Kay Hamilton, Joe Mack Hamilton, and Shirley Brown pose at Leah's grave. Author's collection.

Shirley Brown reads a poem at Leah's grave. Author's collection.

Leah's tombstone discovered. Author's collection.

Cooper tools found on Leah's grave. Author's collection.

Beginning of the road leading to the Betsy Daily Cemetery. Here, Kay, Mack and Shirley come back up the hill after the visit to Leah's grave. Author's collection.

or a lucky buckeye. He calls dragonflies snake doctors and is convinced they cure snakes when they are ill. There is no call to scoff at the beliefs of the Seminole when rural Americans hold just as many superstitious beliefs.[88]

Washoe Native American Practices

The Washoe Indians of Nevada attribute skills and abilities to power. A man who dreamed of rabbits and antelope was more than skillful or lucky because he was endowed with power. The shaman was a man whose special power was the ability to diagnose and cure illness. Illness might come from three sources. A ghost might be angry because some piece of his property was being used by the living, causing him to make sick the user. A sorcerer might cause an illness by using magic to "shoot" a foreign body into his victim. Or a person might become ill because he violated a taboo, such as mistreating pine nuts or pinon trees. To cure the ill, a shaman would be called on to perform a ceremony over the patient. The cure was thought to be brought about not by the shaman's skill but by his power. The power to be a shaman was not sought by the Washoe; rather, it was visited on him. It came unsought and unwelcomed. The power would often come about in dreams where the shaman would dream of an owl, a bear, a ghost, or some other being that would offer power and assistance in life. Sometimes, a young man would ignore the offers of spiritual power, but a spirit being (*wegelayo*) frequently refused to be ignored.

Shamans were considered to be potential sorcerers. Their power was neither good nor bad by itself but could be used for any purpose. One shaman went into a trance during a curing ceremony and fell into a fire that burned his trousers completely away; he, however, was unharmed by the blaze. On his way home, he stopped at a stream to bathe and fell into a faint. When he awoke, the water babies (diminutive water spirits) were taking him to their king, who lived under the water in a great house of stone. He was entertained by five young girls who taught him a song. Later, he was taken by his water baby guides back to where they found him, and he came to, floating on the water.

The most dangerous task for a shaman was retrieving the soul of a person thought to have died. If the shaman's *wegelayo* would lend aid, the shaman could go to the land of the dead and bring back the soul of the person who had died. However, if the soul had drunk from the spring in the land of the dead, it was lost forever. The land of the dead was a happy place where the dead played games, gambled, and danced, unless they had committed a murder. Murderers were banned by the other spirits to another area in a kind of heavenly coventry.

Shamans could be male or female, and the training was the same for both. Their power was not considered exclusively a gift to human beings but was endowed to all things; therefore, just to get through life, each Washoe needed some supernatural help. This general power was extended to all living and inanimate things.

The Washoe feared the spirits of the dead. They were not considered benign things that were concerned with the happiness of the living; rather, they were vengeful and angry; if their property was misused or their burial was not properly conducted or for any one of a dozen other sins of commission or omission, they would come back to haunt the living. Therefore, Washoe funerals were not ceremonies to honor the dead but to make sure the dead person would not return. To ensure the dead did not return, his or her house was burned, and his belongings were burned or buried with him. A prayer invoked the dead to accept their death and leave the living alone.

In Washoe mythology, there was a one-eyed, one-legged giant named Hangwuiwui, a giant bird named Ang that carried people off, and a lecherous coyote that tried to seduce Indian women. The Washoe also believed that in the mountains lived a race of human-like wild men with great strength who caused the disappearance of many people. Many times these wild people would attack humans to get their food.[89]

Apache Native American Practices

The Apache believed that they came from an island to the east that was ravaged by a fire dragon, and they retreated to underground tunnels (caves), carrying the seeds from plants. They emerged and made a home in the desert areas of Arizona and New Mexico. The Apache had medicine men who healed the sick and injured. Sometimes these men specialized in one form of healing or another, such as removing bullets or arrow heads. The Apache bury their dead, while the Yuma practice cremation. Yuma and Apache practice fast-traveling magic. In 1871, an army troop found it necessary to send a courier to Fort Yuma with dispatches, a distance of about ninety miles. They sent an Apache runner, and three days later when they arrived at the fort, they found that the runner had made the mountainous run in thirteen hours, at a rate of about seven miles an hour. The Apache women can carry enormous loads long distances without stopping. This was demonstrated once by an Apache woman, who carried three hundred pounds of bulky hay on her back for four miles or more up a mountain road without resting. The hay was weighed before she left, and the road had been well measured. Other such miraculous feats have been seen.

To combat their ailments, they have medicine men, and most all of the Apache are fond of tattooing, both men and women. The most barbaric forms of witchcraft have been practiced by them. Among the Apache, the men are never accused of the crime, but at extremely long and rare intervals, a woman in a village that has seen more than its share of misfortune is accused of being a witch. Any man woman or child can bear witness against the witch, and the chief of the band acts as the prosecutor. The complaints against the accused are almost always believed once she is charged. The whole village is called to the trial, which almost always leads to an execution. If found guilty, the woman is taken away, stripped to her waist, tied by her thumbs from a tree or rack, and beaten with willow and mesquite branches. This switching of the witch goes on until she faints. It begins again and continues until the executioners themselves are exhausted. If she makes a confession, she is beaten to death with stones; otherwise, she is switched to death. Ordinarily, the Apache have an elaborate funeral ceremony that takes a few days, the men and women mourning with cries similar to a dove cooing. The witch is not afforded these favors. The family is allowed to take the body and bury it, providing the family does not insult the superstitious dignity of the tribe.

The Apache has a supernatural dread of water. They do not use canoes and seldom eat fish. Neither do they eat birds unless they are in starvation conditions, then they prefer the wild turkey over other fowl. No part of a slain animal goes unused, even to the smallest bone.[90]

The Apache war chief Geronimo was a medicine man, very skilled at removing bullets and arrows from his patients. He was known to be precognitive and could accurately foretell the future. He did this when he was on a raiding party one hundred twenty miles from the base camp. While eating, he suddenly stopped and said the base camp had been taken by the white soldiers. The Apache broke camp and started moving that night. Geronimo told his men that in three days a man would stand on a mountain to their left and call out that the camp has been taken. Sure enough, in three days a lone warrior appeared on a hill to the left and shouted that the camp had been taken. There were also other instances that proved Geronimo possessed supernatural powers.[91]

We can see by looking at some of the myths, legends, and belief systems of these five Native American nations that, although they vary, they are relatively consistent across the United States. In one way or another, witchcraft is occasionally practiced, and it usually is a negative practice and punishable. It is interesting that many medicine men are thought to be invested with a power and knowledge through training that can be used for good or evil purposes. Indian Joe knew this information and perhaps shared it with Leah or recognized Leah for a healer and one so invested with power. Certainly, they held a mutual respect for one and another, and it could be that Leah helped preserve a place for Indian Joe on which he built his cabin. She may have foretold his arrival at Staples.

The scope of Native American beliefs is wide-ranging, but generally there is a mystical belief in little people that can be good or bad, in ghosts that haunt the earth and go on to a place of rest, and in witchcraft, in which men and women may become a witch. Lycanthropy in the form of shapeshifters and changers also exists. A form of animism is present, as well as legends of great beasts, water spirits, wild men, and underground dwellers. All of these beliefs have universal distribution, albeit with differences in name and form in Western Europe, as well as America. It is reasonable to believe that Leah Smock's friend Indian Joe taught Leah about these things and that she reciprocated with stories her mother told and passed down the old country.

Contemporary Witchcraft Events from 1813:
Occurrences in Kentucky, Tennessee, and Louisiana

Barren County, Kentucky, 1813

The environment of the frontier was a frightening one. There were American Indians and wild animals, as well as rapids, waterfalls, cliffs, and swamps to traverse. There were few churches or schools and little formal education. Medicine was one step removed from medieval practices, but the desire to have a home and make a living in a strange and sometimes hostile land overcame fears. The beliefs and superstitions that were brought from the Old Country to the English colonies were carried into the frontier. From 1812 through 1815, the United States was at war, fighting England and an Indian alliance formed by the Shawnee war chief Tecumseh. From 1815 until the Indian Removal Act, sporadic fighting with Indian raiding parties occurred throughout Kentucky and Indiana. It was approximately four to six years after the removal of Indians to west of the Mississippi River when Elizabeth and John Smock brought their family from Indiana to Kentucky. All of the superstitious beliefs of Indian and whites were alive and well in the pioneer community. The Indian supernatural customs and beliefs lingered in the pioneer communities due to intermarriage between whites and Indians, and those individual Indians who, for whatever reason, decided to stay or were unaffected by the removal process.

The belief in witches was very much alive in the 1800s. Many times, weather (tornadoes, earthquakes, storms, and drought) and natural events (lightening striking a barn, hens stopping laying eggs, a cow going dry, or a well drying up) were reasons to cast blame. Sometimes, there were people in the community who became targets for that blame. A man with an evil temper, an old crone living alone on the edge of town, or someone considered woodsy or perhaps odd might find themselves accused of causing that calamity because they were suspected to have witched or hexed someone's chicken, cow, or barn. They might well be accused of witchcraft if the community or someone in it had experienced a slight or had a dispute with them before the calamity happened.

In December of 1813, a witchcraft trial was held in a part of Barren County, Kentucky, that is now part of Hart County. The story of this trial was written in 1920 by a Mr. Cyrus Edwards and was published in a book by his daughter, Frances Gardiner, after his death. On August 6, 1803, a Baptist Church was established at what is now Woodsenville, Kentucky, in Barren County, by Elders Jacob Locke, Alexander Davidson, Thomas Whitman, and John Murphy. On April 15, 1804, Mary Reynolds was received as a member of the church on credit of a letter. Five months and one week later, on January 13, 1805, Mrs. Reynolds appeared before the church and complained that three members of the church had accused her publicly of being a witch and using witchcraft.

In those days, the church met on a monthly basis, and the accusers were required to present themselves at the February meeting. Two of her accusers appeared and reiterated the charge. The accuser, a woman, refused to give her reasons for the accusation or retract the claim. At her own request, she asked to be removed from the church rolls. A second accuser, Mr. Thomas Logsdon, being a man of moral courage and strong conclusions, maintained his charge and gave his reasons.

Note: Although the exact accusations against Mrs. Reynolds were not recorded at this meeting, the whole affair caused a great dispute in the church, and partisans from each side accused the other of wrongdoing. At a later meeting, Logsdon made further charges, which he could not prove to the satisfaction of the church, and he was excluded from the rolls. Mrs. Reynolds was then charged with criminal and contradictory statements and at a subsequent meeting was acquitted of all charges. It was believed by all the matter had ended. The excitement in the church extended to the entire community, but what was thought to be the conclusion of the matter proved to be just the beginning.

It was now charged that Logsdon, a man of moral character and standing and of great power for good in the church by his godly example, being a man devoted to his own interests and a poor man, had been railroaded out of the church in disgrace, while the witch had, by the corrupt influence of a few aristocrats (wealthy people), been acquitted. He argued that the reason for the exclusion of each was for intemperate speech, and the charge of witchcraft was never investigated. Throughout the summer and fall, the battle raged, and both sides of the issue increased the strength of their positions. There essentially were two camps: one that believed Mrs. Reynolds was a witch and one that did not. The camp believing her to be a witch had more votes in the church, but those believing her to be innocent had the bulk of learning and intelligence and the sympathy of those of like minds in other churches in the vicinity.

The first fight was that of jurisdiction, and the moderator ruled that the church's Articles of Faith included no power to have a trial on charges of witchcraft. The majority side who believed she was a witch demanded that the church take a definite position by the next meeting and that the question was propounded as an article of faith and ruled by a majority vote. The following question was to be voted on: "Is it consistent with Divinity for the followers of Jesus Christ to believe there is such a thing as supernatural witchcraft, or to encourage the same belief?" If the vote was in the affirmative, Mrs. Reynolds would be tried for witchcraft.

Reverend Locke did not believe in witchcraft but maintained as the church leader a neutral stance between the two factions, not apparently taking sides. There was intense interest in this fight, not only in the Baptist churches but also in other churches around the area. Many sermons were preached on the subject, and on the fourth Saturday in December 1813, the battle lines were drawn. During all this time, Reverend Locke, in spite of his disbelief in witchcraft, maintained the confidence and admiration of both sides. He had postponed this meeting in the hopes that cooler minds would prevail, and he prepared a speech in which he wished intelligence and education would win over superstition. He felt a decision otherwise would cause a disgrace to fall over the Barren and Green River area.

The faction that believed Reynolds was a witch suffered organizational difficulty. It had no titular head. There were three leaders of that faction: Mr. Peter Rowlett, Thomas Woodson, and Richard J. Munford. On the day of the trial, Reverend Locke spoke from the front doors of the church to the large assembly seated on benches out-of-doors. The day was a fair, warm Indian Summer day. This meeting was likely the largest group of people to assemble in the county at one time to hear a sermon. There were people from Glasgow, Knob Lick, Lafayette, Silent Grove, and Nolin attending. There were many preachers from Baptist, Methodist, and Presbyterian churches in the crowd. Reverend Locke was knowledgeable about history and the Bible and was skilled in oration and logic. He was at the zenith of his abilities when he preached that day. He preached for three hours and swayed many voters to his view. The next day, a vote was quietly taken, and the belief in witchcraft was voted down. However, a number of people withdrew from the church, including large families. Those that remained disavowed witchcraft, but those that left continued their belief, and do yet today.[92]

Tennessee's Bell Witch, 1817

Certainly one of best-known cases of witchcraft is the Bell Witch of Tennessee. Some psychic investigators believe this is more of a case of haunting than witchcraft, but as we have seen, the two seem inextricably linked together.

The Bells were Baptist and raised their children in the faith. They lived good Christian lives and were exemplary citizens of their community. John and his wife Lucy were married and had eight children. It all began in 1817 when John Bell, walking through his cornfield, was confronted by an animal, somewhat dog-like, the visage of which he had never seen. He raised his gun and shot at the creature, and it vanished before his eyes. A few days later, he saw a bird he thought to be a turkey sitting on a fence, but when it flew away, he saw it was of immense size and like no bird he had seen before. At about the same time in the Bell house, the family regularly heard knockings and scrapings on the walls. Covers were pulled off the beds, and dishes flew about the house. Occupants of the house were slapped by spectral hands, their hair pulled. The Bell children seemed to become targets of the witch. William Bell, the youngest child, was six when the events first happened, Joel and Drury Bell were older, and his sister Elizabeth was twelve, while John Junior was twenty-four. Another child, Bennet, had died, and Zadok was away practicing law. Jesse and Esther were married and had moved nearby. Periodically the Bell Witch manifested itself as a bird, a rabbit or a dog. Eventually, the witch began to make herself or himself vocally known. Unintelligible utterances soon became whispers and could be understood. At first, it spoke only at night, and later it would speak at all hours of the day or night. Once it said, "I am a spirit from everywhere: Heaven, Hell, the Earth. I'm in the air, in houses, any place, any time. I've been created millions of years. That is all I will tell you." It declared another time, "I am a spirit. I was once very happy but have been disturbed. I am the spirit of a person buried in the woods nearby, and the grave has been disturbed, my bones disinterred and scattered, and one of my teeth was lost under the house. I'm here looking for that tooth."[93] Since an Indian burial ground was located nearby, a search was made for the tooth, to no avail. The witch made fun of them for searching and, finally, proved to scoff at their efforts and to tease and make fun of them. Eventually, the witch identified herself as Kate Batts, a witch. She could quote scripture from the Bible fluently. She would sometimes accompany the Bells to prayer meeting, where she would thump under the chairs. Soon, Kate introduced the Bells to other members of her family of four: Blackdog, who spoke in a harsh feminine voice; Mathematics and Cypocryphy, who had softer feminine voices; and Jerusalem, who spoke like a boy.[94] They were invisible but visibly manifested themselves by walking through brush or weeds, which would move to the sides as they passed through unseen. They used profanity. The witching continued for three years, and eventually, John Bell was found in a coma. There was a strange vial of a black liquid in the medicine cabinet. Kate said out loud, "I've given old Jack a big dose of it and fixed him." John Bell died December 20, 1820. Betsy continued to be tormented, and her engagement with her boyfriend was called off. Finally, the witch announced, "I am leaving now and won't be back for seven years." She manifested in a visible ball of smoke and fire that came out of the chimney. Eventually, the Bell house was torn down, and she did not return.[95] Now, the cave on the property is a tourist attraction that draws many visitors each year.

New Orleans, 1819

Marie Laveau was born September 10, 1801 to biracial parents. She was Creole. Marie married Jacques Paris August 4, 1819 and had a daughter Marie Laveau II, who was called Paris after Marie's husband. Marie and her daughter were both thought to be witches of high order, but the first Marie, not unlike Leah Smock and her mother Elizabeth, was thought to be the more powerful of the two. They practiced a form of witchcraft that likely migrated to the Western Hemisphere with the West African slave trade, known as *vodoun*. Later, this term became known as voodoo, likely a white corruption of the original name. Voodoo is a combination of Roman Catholicism and West African native beliefs, including magic. It has similarities to other religions, such as Santeria, but by comparison is much more benign. It was brought to the United States with the importation of slaves. Between 1794 and 1804, a revolution in Haiti caused emigration to Louisiana and other areas of the South. This emigration also caused an increase in the number of people who practiced voodoo. With that growth, it caused jealousy and enmity between rival practitioners or witches. There could be some connection, admittedly tenuous, between these practices and those of the Salem, Massachusetts slave girl Tituba in 1692. Fiona Goode, a relative and perhaps a granddaughter of Sarah Good from Salem, had moved to New Orleans and not only knew but also conversed with Marie Laveau. During the Salem trials, the Parris family was one of the factions, and of course, Marie's husband was named Paris. Some say Marie and Sarah Good were friends, while others say they were enemies. The connections, coincidental or not, between Salem's witches and Marie Laveau are tantalizing.

Marie was known to be an importer of liquor, and she was a hair dresser to some of the aristocratic, well-to-do, fashionable New Orleans women. It was through the servants and slaves of these wealthy women that she may have received personal information about her clients that she used when she gave them private readings, potions, and advice.

Not a lot is known about Marie's magical ability, but she was reputed to be a healer who knew the use of herbs and poisons. She was accused of poisoning a rival witch. There have been accusations that she raised the dead (or their spirits) and conversed with them as a necromancer. She was said to possess ESP, and she could move objects without touching them.

Marie Laveau was known by some to be a vengeful woman, harboring grudges and animosity against rival witches. One rather significant display of her power happened when an execution by hanging was supposed to take place. A relative of the man to be hanged contracted with Marie to keep the man from dying on the gallows. Anecdotal evidence states when the trap was sprung, the rope broke, and the victim was saved. Marie was reputed to have a pet snake named Zombie after an African deity. She died June 15, 1881 at the age of eighty. Many reports were given by people who said she appeared to them, much like Leah Smock, after her death. Some think that sparked the printing of her obituary June 16, 1881, announcing that she had died peacefully in her sleep. The legend of Marie Laveau is alive and well today. Decades ago, a rumor stated that if you went to Marie's tomb and drew an X on it, made a wish, turned around three times, and knocked on the tomb, the wish would be granted. When it came to pass, you had to return and circle the X. Many people make pilgrimages to her tomb, and someone on or about December 13, 2013 painted her tomb pink.

Paranormal researcher and New Orleans area historian Danielle Stump explained that it's hard today getting people to discuss Marie. Some are fearful of her spirit, and others do not discuss her out of respect. The area is still very superstitious, and the practice of voodoo is still alive there. Danielle explains that Marie did not peddle curses when she was alive, although she did sell love potions that were custom made to bring out the individual customers' pheromones. Her prosperity potions contained roots and plants that enhance energy, memory, and brain function, all the things one needed to become or remain prosperous. Above all, she was a healer. Her success was greater than those of the doctors in the area. She was known to charge only those persons with the ability to pay for her services. Everything she did was with a flare: religious rituals, music, dance, and snakes, while embracing a blend of Catholicism and voodoo. Danielle states that her husband Paris died six months after he disappeared and her marriage to him. She relates that Marie's fifteen children were fathered by a man named Christopher Glapion. Marie, being Catholic, believed in marrying only once in a lifetime.[96] Whatever Marie was—healer, witch, or voodoo priestess—she certainly left her mark on New Orleans, and her legacy is as alive today as is Leah Smock's is in Battletown. I think it is important to note that, just like the influence Native Americans may have had on Leah, directly or indirectly through Indian Joe, there were many slaves in Meade County who would likely have introduced the West African beliefs they carried with them into their slave quarters. River commerce between New Orleans and Meade County, Kentucky, was active during the 1830s through the early 1940s, and there were many slaves in and around Battletown.

Witches in 1829 Sentenced to burn in Paducah, Kentucky

In 1829 on the banks of the Ohio River, a large fire was made of brush and timber, and two women who were found guilty of witchcraft were thrown into the fire. They made their way out of the fire only to be thrown in once again. After their second time to exit the flames, the large crowd that gathered to watch objected, and the women were set free. It is believed their surname was Craft, and according to a Mrs. F. C. Mocquot, who wrote a story about the incident based on a handwritten manuscript, these women lived in a "hovel" near the confluence of the Ohio and Clark's Rivers. Author Berry Craig explains in a December 1986 article in the *Kentucky Explorer* that Gip Husbands owned the manuscript, and it was found by Reverend Rogers when Husbands died. J. C. Copeland had a photo copy of the original.

A man who lived in McCracken County believed the women had bewitched him and had them arrested for witchcraft. The fact that they were arrested is evidence there was a law on the books prohibiting witchcraft or that the superstitions were strong enough to let the Biblical verse "suffer not a witch to live" to stand as law. The original text was "suffer not a poisoner to live" but was changed in the King James version of the Bible, and this was the basis for the colonial law applied to the Salem witch executions.

Craig raises the question of whether there were Kentucky laws prohibiting witchcraft. There may not have been, he states, but there were such trials in Virginia, and since Kentucky was once part of the "Old Dominion," Virginia common law might have been license enough to try and convict the women. He mentions a Monroe County man named Montell who said in 1929 a Cumberland County, Kentucky man accused a woman of being a witch because when she got mad at his wife, her hens quit laying eggs, and when he became the target of her wrath, his cow gave bloody milk.[97]

Curiously, in 1929, three men were sentenced for the murder of one witch by another. Two men received a life sentence and one a prison term.

An 1831 Case of Witchcraft in Letcher County, Kentucky

A woman by the name of Tabatha Boggs was said to be a witch who could charm guns, dogs, and other animals. Tabatha gave birth to a son named Bill Boggs. Boggs was said to live on a hill in Letcher County and would fire his gun at the sun, cursed, and blessed until the ground would tremble and shake and thunder began to peal. It was said if a person could stand the fear of all this, they would become a witch.

In Rowan County, Kentucky, John A. Black, who was said to be a witch and a shapeshifter, died. He was believed to practice black magic and could change his form to that of any animal. Legend has it that John was killed by his youngest son, Willie, while John was in the form of a huge black dog that was chasing Willie's horse. This dog had chased Willie's mare before, and Willie was determined to keep the dog from getting the horse. He must have considered the dog to be of supernatural order because he made a bullet of a silver coin and shot the dog. The legend states when the dog was shot, it turned back into the form of John Black, and he died a gruesome death a few days later.

According to this story, shapeshifting or skin-changing is a trait of male Kentucky witches. As we have seen in Part I of this book, early witches in Western Europe were thought to change into animals because of the various animal skins, hides, and horns or antlers they wore at their nocturnal ceremonies and dances. Witches were said to have kissed the male wizard under his tail as a tribute. It is true that American witch traditions don't normally associate skin changing or shapeshifting to witches, but there are those Native American traditions allowing for the practice. And although familiars are said to be part of the European witch tradition, could these have been considered spirits that took animal form?

Chapter 11

LEAH SMOCK COUNTRY

S ome thirty-six years after Squire Boone vacated Kentucky for good, the Smock family settled in what was to be called Battletown, Kentucky. At the time of the Leah Smock burning, Battletown was a community of residences named Staples or Stapleton. In 1840, it was a very remote and secluded community. A wilder and less-settled part of Staples was known as Lapland. That area continues to be known as Lapland today. However, Battletown was not named that until 1885, when Mack J. Bennett, an ancestor of "Cowboy" Bennett, the expert on the lore of Leah Smock, tried to get a post office established in the hamlet of Staples. Mack Bennett owned a general store located on Wolf Creek Road. He made application for the post office. But the United States Postal Department had refused to accept the proposed name, Staples, because there was another office in the state by the same name. Mr. Bennett had to submit another name. During the time the new name was being decided, two men had a fight over a gun and whiskey dispute in front of the store. The two men in the fight were Jim Bennett and a Mr. Hubbard. Mack Bennett, amused by the fight and possessing a sense of humor, decided to submit the name Battletown, Kentucky. It was accepted by the postal authorities.

The area of Battletown is rich in deep limestone deposits, and the lime kiln industry, which processed the stone to make lime for agricultural purposes, developed in the area. This meant that barrels were needed, and the coopers (barrel makers) became especially important to the area because the processed lime was placed in barrels for shipment to the landings and farms. Leah Smock's father was a cooper and may have been attracted to the region because of a ready market for his trade and the raw material available to make them, but for whatever reason, he settled there.

The Smock Family

Leah's father, John Smock, was born in New Jersey on May 16, 1797. He married Margaret Anne, whose maiden name is unknown. Margaret was born in Pennsylvania in 1796, the exact location unknown. Her father was from Scotland. Margaret and John had three children. Their first child, Leah, was born in January of 1818, perhaps in Virginia where the Smocks lived before moving to Kentucky. While in Virginia, Margaret gave birth to a boy, Joseph T. Smock, about 1825. John, Margaret, Leah, and Joseph moved to Washington County, Kentucky, where they are listed in the 1830 census. By 1835, they were living in Indiana near New Amsterdam, where Elizabeth Ann, their last child, was born on July 26, 1835. In 1840, a John Smock is listed by the census in Washington County, which abuts Marion County; however, this John Smock was listed as the head of a household with nine male children and may be a different man but possibly related. We do know John Smock was in Meade County before November 26, 1839 because he purchased three hundred acres of land from an agent, Ben Hardin, representing the Colstron estate. The land had previously been sold to John Greer, as shown by bond for a deed made part hereof and filed as No. 78, in a lawsuit executed in Meade Circuit Court, by William Leigh, executor of Plaintiff R. Colstron est., against John Smock and others, Defendant.

John Smock stated in his answer to the suit that the…

> Greer purchase covers all of the land he purchased except for a few poles. He is willing to the contract with this defendant shall be rescinded and his note cancelled and given up, but if this may not be done then he asks that the Plaintiff and said Greer implead and settle the rights of Greer and said collections before he be compelled to pay anything on said notes. He says if said plaintiff shall show his ability to convey the land when this defendant shall pay for it then he owes the notes. He asks under the circumstances a rescission of the contract and the notes be cancelled and for such orders and judgments as to equity and justice belong and for all proper relief.

> For Defendant
> John Smock says he believes the statements of the forgoing answers are true.

Sworn to before me by John Smock. This 26th day of November, 1839.

A. T. Rankin

So, it seems that for a period of five years from 1830 until 1835, John
Smock and his family were residing for a time in Kentucky and Indiana. Smock was to pay for the three hundred acres of land, purchased
from the Rawleigh Colstron Estate, in three equal payments, one third
in 1840, one third in 1841, and the final third in 1842. This manner of
payment was commonplace for farms in Kentucky, even as late as the
mid-1950s.[98] The terms of the mortgage usually gave the buyers one
year to get a crop in before the first payment was due, which means
that the Smock land may have been purchased sometime between
1837 and 1838. The suit was filed November 26, 1839, at least a year
after the purchase, giving time for John Smock to find out the land
had been previously sold to John Greer and in time for him to default
on making the first payment. Since the suit didn't ask for the return
of any payment, we can assume that no payment had been made. According to the family papers of Shirley Brown, it states, "In the famous
Court case of Rawleigh Colstron vs John Smock & others dated May
24, 1839"[99] (Note: The original paper had the date 1859, which seems
obviously to be a date error.)

Ben Hardin, the agent for the Rawleigh R. Colstron Estate, was reputed to have sold the land to both John Greer and to John Smock.
The suit was initiated on May 24, 1839[100]. Thus, we can deduce that the
latest date for the purchase would be May 1838 and perhaps a while before that. John Smock was either living in Staples or visiting the area in
search of land to buy before 1838. No one can say with certainty when
the Smocks began residing in Meade County, but it was not before July
of 1835 when Elizabeth Anne was born in Indiana. Sometime during a
three year period, the Smocks crossed the Ohio River and began residing near what is now Battletown, Kentucky.

The land that John Smock bought consisted of three hundred acres,
largely wooded and dense. He may have needed the wooded land to
provide raw material for his cooperage operation. There may have
been a house and barn on the land when it was purchased, but there
is evidence that in 1842 there was a house, barn, smokehouse or drying room, and a cooperage in the barn or in another building sepa-

rate from the barn. It is safe to assume there was an outhouse, chicken house, and perhaps a shed or two. John Smock's land contained the Betsy Daily Cemetery, and the first person buried in that cemetery was Leah Smock.

"In the 1843 tax list we find John Smock is taxed for three hundred acres of land. On November 22, 1843, we find, 'I assine (sic) the within bond to Johnston Bennett' it is signed by John Smock. The bond is for three hundred acres of land he had purchased from Ben Hardin. In other tax lists at later dates, he is listed for being taxed for fifty acres of land. In 1861, we find John Smock bought fifty acres of land from Richard (Dixon) Chism and his wife Elizabeth. This land is located today on Wolf Creek Road (Hwy. 228) going west toward Wolf Creek on the farm where Raymond Wesley and Mabel Chism lived. Ironically, the acreage John Smock bought in Wolf Creek is presently viewable from Leah's great-great-niece Shirley Brown's house, on a hill that overlooks his land. This was known first as the Smock Place, and later Ballard Place; their daughter married first Israel Allen then later Blanford Ballard.

"In 1872, John Smock wrote his last will and testament. John died Feb. 11, 1876 and is buried in the Cunningham Family Cemetery, located on Ursel Singleton's farm at Wolf Creek. Margaret died June 3, 1889. This taked (sic) from a family Bible. There is no mention of where she is buried, possibly beside her daughter Leah or maybe by her husband and other daughter Elizabeth. Elizabeth died October 18, 1882 and is also buried in the Cunningham Cemetery.

We have no record of their son Joseph T. Smock ever marrying. In 1860, he was thirty-four years of age and living with his parents. It also states he was a steam boatman. Nothing is known of him after 1872 when his father's will mentions "son, Joseph T."

The following statements are anecdotal as told by several elderly people who lived in the Battletown area: "Margaret was considered a very remarkable person. It is told that she had some sort of healing powers and proved the same on several occasions."[101] "Some say she was a powerful witch."

Leah Smock was murdered August 21, 1840 at home, where she lived with her parents, John and Margaret, her brother John, and her sister Elizabeth for two or three years. She was burned to death at the age of twenty-two years and seven months. It is because of her mysterious death at the hands of her neighbors that she has been immortalized.

She is also legendary because since her death she has refused to leave the area of Battletown, and from time to time, she appears to people in a white gown, surrounded by a purple mist with cords tied at her waist, wrists, and neck. She makes herself known in many other ways.

Since Leah likely did not live continuously in Meade County for more than three years and perhaps for only two, she made a pronounced impression on the inhabitants of the people in Battletown in a relatively short period of time. It is possible she lived sporadically in Staples while John was searching for land. It is obvious that some of the stories about Leah occurred when she was at the tender age of ten or twelve. These stories that are now part of her legend were either told to the ancestors of those who repeat them today or related by her family members or even Leah herself. In 1838, her sister Elizabeth Anne would have been three years old and her brother Joseph about thirteen years of age. Leah would have been eighteen or nineteen and likely the primary helper of her mother and father.

Chapter 12
LEAH SMOCK'S STORY

T he story of Leah is shrouded in mystery, as dark, indiscernible, and secret as the wooded hills and hollows of old Lapland. The area is known for the lovely, mysterious girl said to be a witch and the venomous snakes that infest the place. I was once told by a man who knew the area well that he would guide me to the site of Leah's grave but only after the first killing frost had driven the rattlesnakes and copperheads deep underground. Even then, he suggested we carry side arms just in case. To get to the Betsy Daily Cemetery, there are two routes, neither of which is easy. To follow the first route, you must turn off the road and drive a mile or so, then walk for nearly a mile, partially through a dry creek bed, until you get to the dark, secluded, and forested place where some eighty pioneer settlers are buried. That's the easy route. To the far side of the cemetery, away from most of the stones, many of them covered by "mourning ivy," pine needles, and leaves, lies the grave of Leah. Many people have tried to transplant the ivy, but by the time they get home, they find the ivy plants have disappeared. Those plants that have made it home die soon after transplanting. The stones are not all carved; some of them are simple field stones, just marker enough so people will know where not to walk. The cemetery itself began with Leah's grave, the oldest there. Her mother, Margaret, may lie at Leah's side. The cemetery was used from 1840 to about 1920, some eighty odd years, when, for whatever reason, it was abandoned, except for decoration days. Now it is closed, and the property is inaccessible to the public.

A reporter who visited the site said he was stricken at the sight of the grave. He described the witch's grave as ominous: "It seemed to be giving off vibrations of a time long ago, marred with mystery and misfortune." The rocks that had been placed upon the grave have been strewn about. Souvenir hunters have taken some of them. Despite their efforts to keep Leah in her grave, the witch woman has reappeared from time to time to haunt hunters or visitors to the cemetery. The animals in the graveyard are almost tame, and though many animals are in the vicinity of the cemetery, no hunter has been able to bring any down. Leah was said to have an affinity with the animals, and she loved the wild things. She could tame even high-spirited animals or ones that had bitten their masters.

There are many legends about the cemetery, and some evidence exists at the grave site that at least one of the stories is true. After Leah was burned alive, she was buried by her family, the young man who loved her, perhaps Indian Joe, and a few girlfriends. A short while after the burial, her mother, also a witch, told some neighbors that she had spoken to Leah when her daughter's apparition appeared at the place where she was burned. A second person with Leah's mother on that occasion also witnessed her apparition. Leah's mother said then, and for many years thereafter, "They shouldn't have treated Leah that way." She was also known to say she "couldn't understand why Leah did not use her powers to escape her fate." A week or two after Leah's burial, a hunter in the vicinity of the cemetery was looking for game when he saw Leah's incomplete form standing, looking down at her grave. She was as beautiful in death as she was in life, but her form stopped short of the ground. She was dressed in a long-sleeved white robe that had ruffles at the wrist and was tied with black cord or rope at the wrist, neck, and waist. The cord around her waist was tied with the ends hung down. Her hair was long, below her shoulders, and wafted in the gentle breeze. The birds and the animals did not make a sound, and the cemetery was eerily quiet. The hunter quickly left and reported to the neighbors what he had seen. Three weeks after she was buried, two weeks or so after the sighting, a party of men got together two wagons loaded with sandstone rocks and drove them to the cemetery. There, they took wooden shovels and spades and dug down into the recently-filled grave to her coffin. They took the stones, large and small, and filled the grave with them, stacking them three feet above the grave. They did not want Leah to arise and avenge her death upon them. They were afraid.

Leah was a bright, pretty girl with coal-black eyes and long raven-black hair. She was tolerable slender with a natural build and a fair face. She was a lovely girl and a beautiful woman. Although not much is known about her religious ideas, she was from a Christian home, though her mother was suspected of practicing sorcery. "She was pretty religious in a way. She said a bedtime prayer, as all children were taught to do in those days," said "Cowboy" Bennett, but she worshipped the "old way."

Leah's gravestone was shaped and engraved by her lover, a man lesser known even than Leah. All we know is his age, twenty-five, and that he possibly carved Leah a serpentine rod or walking stick that she carried into the woods on her treks there, though others say it was carved by Leah's friend, Indian Joe. Her boyfriend obviously loved her because he took some time to choose just the right stone that he set on her grave after he shaped the stone and expertly carved the words:

LEAH SMOCK
DEPARTED THIS LIFE
1840
AGE 22 YEARS 7 MONTHS

In 1830 when Leah was about twelve years of age, she was recognized to be a very intelligent girl, imbued with knowledge beyond her years. Like Jesus discussing law in the temple with the priests and rabbis, she could hold a conversation with adults on any subject and speak with the authority of her convictions. It was at this time that Leah began to draw attention in a queer way. Even today, many old people won't speak of her, and if they do, it's in hushed tones, and it took years for the man who chronicled her history, "Cowboy" Bennett, to piece together the tale. The old people who knew the story were afraid to talk for fear they would be witched or haunted by Leah.

Although Leah was eighteen or nineteen when she came to live in the wilds of Meade County, the people of Lapland became aware that Leah was no ordinary child and that she possessed special powers. The stories of her psychic abilities, said to be inherited from her mother, were told and retold by the people of Lapland. They said that she witched things. Leah was known to be intelligent, possessing a high I.Q. She was at the head of her class in the schools she attended, likely in Virginia. It was rare that a child of twelve could speak intellectually with adults, but Leah could. The neighbors, wherever the Smocks resided, began to notice something even more puzzling about the young, dark-haired girl. She could foretell events with uncanny accuracy and predict the weather and details about the seasons in advance. She could tell if a sick person would get well or die, and Leah was known to contradict some of the doctors who treated people in the community, saying their patients would improve or die, and no matter what the doctors said, whatever Leah said came to pass. At first, this ability impressed and awed the people, but later it led them to fear her, and they wouldn't let their children associate with Leah. Probably out of fear, ignorance, or jealousy, the people began to ridicule and scorn her.

Leah recoiled at this treatment and seemed to lash out at those who chose to shun her. Some people asked her to bewitch their crops, and when she did, they had bumper harvests. She could make things grow like no other, but when she was mistreated, it was thought she wreaked a vengeance on those who mistreated her, using her powers to get even. She allegedly boasted about her power and play on the fears of the people by cautioning them to not to show their ill will toward her or she would cause things to happen. During any harassment or verbal abuse that was heaped upon her, she would turn slightly away and get a distant look in her eyes. This again and again proved to be a bad omen for those who mistreated or scorned her. One such incident happened when Leah took a fancy to a three-month-old baby who was sick. She asked to hold the baby, but the parents wouldn't let her touch the child. Leah was reported to say, "You'll be sorry by morning." And they were because the child died. Leah returned and tried to touch the child in the coffin, and again she was rebuked. That night, at the home of the deceased child, the dogs howled, the cats were restless on top of the roof, and strange noises were heard all night. Looking outside, the parents saw Leah standing in the dark, with a curious smile on her face. She was taken home by the bereaved father of the child, and the previous occurrences stopped.

Another time, a man had just bought a fine team of horses, and Leah wanted to pet one. The man told her he didn't want her touching his horses and pushed Leah, although Leah did manage to touch one horse on the nose before she was dragged away. The next morning, the horse she touched had died, and the second horse died the next day. In a third instance, a cooper who had chastised her had just completed a full day's work, assembling eighteen barrels. The next day, all of the tacks came out of the barrel rings, and they fell completely apart.

Another incident happened in the vicinity of Wolf Creek when two men wanted to build a log cabin. Leah warned against it, but they went ahead. One man broke his leg during the construction, and another man went crazy. After a part of the house was built, a bad storm came up and blew down all that had been erected. Later on, a young Indian man came along, nicknamed Indian Joe by the whites. When he took a liking to the place, Leah said the place was intended for him. He moved in, built a cabin, and lived there for many years. Leah may have foreseen Indian Joe was coming and was destined to reside there. Not much more is known about Indian Joe. Leah may have first met him around 1835 when she lived in Indiana. Regardless, Indian Joe became a friend of Leah's. Some say he carved her serpentine walking stick that Leah was seen carrying in the fields and forests. *Note: "Cowboy" Bennett, born in 1914, remembered Indian Joe from his childhood. Reputed to be the first person buried in the Cunningham Cemetery, his grave was simply marked with a piece of sandstone rock. He may have been over one hundred years old when he died. If he arrived in 1840 at about the age of sixteen, he would have been ninety years old in 1914, and Bennett, at age five or ten, easily could have remembered him, making Indian Joe ninety-five or one hundred. Of course, Indian Joe could have lived longer.*

Some farmers wanted to use a pond to water their cattle. Leah told them not to do so because their cattle would die. The farmers dug up all the poisonous milkweed and jimson weed, but when the cattle drank from the pond, they all died. Once, two boys began following and teasing Leah for being a witch. Leah, who was often seen walking through the woods in the company of wolves, foxes, and wildcats, had an affinity with animals. On this occasion, she was said to have called up her animal friends, and they began chasing the boys through the woods. Several days later, the boys were found wandering about aimlessly, completely out of their minds. Another version of this story states the children were found dead. Today, the abundance of animals at her grave is noticeable as is the inability of hunters to shoot them. Her spirit seems to watch over them.

Those who mistreated Leah or her family believed they eventually felt her wrath. Crops withered and died, barns and houses burned mysteriously, and the self-confident Leah convinced her neighbors she was a witch. Because of the incidents and maybe the lawsuit, the Smock family became ostracized, and the Lapland residents stopped trading with them. After Leah's death, Bennett says that the Smocks were so looked down upon that they were in a social class by themselves, lower even than the slaves. The Smocks had to move, and John Smock hired himself out as a farm hand. With John taking menial jobs as a farm worker, the Smocks moved about Meade, Breckenridge, and Hancock counties.

Leah had a boyfriend, several girlfriends, and her Indian friend Joe; she was often seen walking the fields and woods with her serpentine rod or staff. She was avoided by people because of the experience the two boys had when they taunted her. No one wanted to tempt fate. Leah was feared, and the fear grew in the collective minds of the people in the community. The final strike against Leah was the charge that, whenever she went into a home with a male baby, a short while later it would die. It was said Leah cast spells. By now, rightfully or wrongfully, the community wanted her gone.

In those days, farm families used a smokehouse or drying room to preserve meat and dry fruits and vegetables. Sometimes, the hams were cured with sugar or salt and smoked. Other times, the pork was salted down and layered in barrels, a layer of salt, a layer of meat, and so on. Apples, pears, and such were cored and sliced and hung up high on strings or rods until they were dried. Beans were often strung by a needle and thread in their pods and dried to become "leather breeches" beans. Of course, herbs such as parsley, sage, and wild garlic (ramps) were hung up and dried. Oftentimes, fires were lit in the smokehouse to cure the meat and to keep the insects (skippers) away. On the Smock place, there was a smokehouse and a cooperage, a shed or barn where Leah and her father made barrels. The floor of the cooperage was always covered in wood shavings from the shaping of the barrel staves. Someplace in the cooperage, there was a forge and a place for a fire because the barrel rings hand to be heated, forged, and welded. Joseph Smock, now fifteen or sixteen years of age, had left home to work on the riverboats, and Leah alone helped her father make barrels. It was at her home that Leah met death.

The Death of Leah Smock

There are four versions of how Leah died, and four different accounts of where she died. Details regarding her death are also a little sketchy with all of the information being anecdotal, and the event happening some 176 years ago. It has been reported that she was starved to death in the woods or that she was hanged, or that she was shot; however, most accounts say she died by fire. The account that asserts she starved to death in the woods is unlikely since Leah would probably be the last person to starve in the woods. She knew the woods as well as the animals, and she certainly knew which plants to eat and which to leave alone. If she did die in that manner, she would have had to be tied, imprisoned, or incapacitated in some way, so she could not get the nourishment the forest provided. There are three places she was said to have burned to death. One story says she died in a house fire, another says she died in a fire in the cooperage, and yet others say she died in the smokehouse. In 1840, dying in a house fire was the second-most frequent cause of death for women, childbirth being the first. If, however, she died in a house fire, that story seems to leave out the neighbors who were supposedly involved in her death and the fact that the Smocks continued to reside on the property, most likely in the house. This leaves the probability that she either died in the smokehouse or the cooperage. The preponderance of anecdotal evidence favors the smokehouse or drying room. Only one written account states she died in the cooperage; likewise, only one story states she died in the house.

One hot August day in 1840, Leah's parents had gone to the nearby village of Staples, which would have meant a wagon ride over rugged roads, up and down steep hills, fording one creek, encompassing a one way trip of three or more miles. Leah remained at home, presumably doing chores in the house, cooperage, or more probably the smokehouse. When her parents had been gone long enough to be out of earshot and were far enough away that they would likely keep going rather than turn back in the event they had forgotten something and unable to see the smoke, an unspecified number of their neighbors came out from hiding and accosted Leah. They tied her hands and perhaps her feet and locked her in the smokehouse, maybe nailing the door shut. These anonymous people then set fire to the place she was in, and she burned to death. They lingered until her screaming stopped, and she mercifully died. Her beautiful body, subjected to the flames, was burned beyond recognition.

On their return, the Smocks probably thought that some tragic accident had befallen their daughter, but eventually talk got around that Leah was purposely burned because she was a witch. Her girlfriends, boyfriend, or Indian Joe were likely the first to hear that she was murdered and relayed that information to John and Margaret. She was taken in her coffin by wagon to what would become the Betsy Daily Cemetery, and on the disputed property of John Smock, she was buried. Since hers was the first grave, it may be that lonely spot was selected since she would undoubtedly not have been welcomed in the churchyard. Her boyfriend carved a headstone for Leah and set it on her grave. Leah Smock was dead and buried, gone forever, or was she?

After Her Burial

The first sighting of Leah came just a few days after she was buried, and that resulted in the filling with stones and covering of her grave, probably by those who set the fire. Soon, more stories of sighting began to circulate. Many years later, newspaper men covering the stories reported on her after-life movements. One *Courier-Journal* newspaper reporter, Bill Osinski, reported, "Here lies Leah Smock…most of the time." And so it was. Many people have reported to have heard pounding and clanging sounds coming from the cemetery, the type of sounds one would expect to come from a cooperage. Occasionally, newly-made barrels would turn up sitting in the cemetery, and on one occasion, a man named Hamilton found cooper's tools on the stones on Leah's grave.

Chapter 13
THE LEGACY OF LEAH

Leah Smock's story has been recounted for many years in Battle-town, Kentucky, but outside of Meade County, her story is largely unknown; however, even today, events happen that are associated with Leah. Once, a television crew wanted to do a remote broadcast from the cemetery on Halloween, October 31, 1991. On that warm, pleasant evening, a two person news crew and fifteen people walked to the cemetery to the witch's grave. The walk to the cemetery was more than a mile from their van, so the film crew, consisting of cameraperson Janine White and news reporter Ezra Marcus, checked the batteries, lights, and cameras before going to the gravesite to ensure the equipment was working prior to filming. On arrival, the reporter was setting up at the grave, and when the lights were needed, they discovered that none of the recently-checked equipment was functioning. Rather than walking back to the van, a decision was made to do the shoot by flashlight. Interestingly, two boys who were holding flashlights had them jerked away by unseen hands. They assumed adults took them for the shoot, but when they asked, no one admitted taking them. A search of the area failed to find their lights. The grandfather of one of the boys was asked to take a seat on the stones upon Leah's grave. He said he felt uncomfortable doing so but acquiesced for the filming. The flashlights of others were used, and the filming and broadcast were successful. When the party arrived back at the van, the lights were found to be functioning perfectly. The news crew could not explain the malfunction at the grave and were mystified.

The next day had turned overcast, and a storm seemed to threaten. The man whose grandson had lost his flashlight received a telephone call from the boy's mother, asking if he would go back and retrieve the boy's coat, which had been left in the cemetery. It was well in the afternoon, so he allowed two hours to drive there, get the coat, and return home before dark. As he got closer to the turnoff, the sky became darker, and the wind blew harder. He drove down the dirt road to the cemetery and walked to the grave; there, he found the boy's coat draped over Leah's tombstone and the flashlight laying on the grave. He grabbed them and walked back to his truck and found it wouldn't start. It began to sleet and rain, and he decided to walk out of the area and seek help. He walked and walked and, after a long time, came directly back to his truck. By now, the temperature dropped, and freezing rain was forming on the metal surfaces of the truck. He tried to open the door to get warm inside but couldn't. Dropping down on his knees in despair and fear, he jumped when he felt a cold hand touch his shoulder. It was his wife and the man, Bean Bennet, who guided him the night before. He told me he thought it possible Leah got even for his sitting on her grave. Maybe it's so.

Once, a retired school teacher I know visited Leah's grave and found a copperhead snake coiled on top of the stones. She watched as it flicked its forked tongue, tasting the air, and then silently slithered beneath the stones into Leah's grave. Two hunters a while ago were hunting deer one evening near the cemetery. When they looked in the direction of Leah's grave, they saw her standing there in her white robe with black ties at her wrist, neck, and waist. She was very pretty with her dark eyes and long raven tresses. She had an aura of purple surrounding her in the darkening forest. Badly frightened, they hurriedly left the area. Other hunters occasionally smell freshly-cut wood or hear the hammering of the barrel-making process coming from the cemetery.

A teacher tells of a class play about Leah Smock that was performed for the students of Battletown Elementary School. Musician Leah Medley played the part of Leah Smock, and her teacher was genealogist Cindy Henning. A smokehouse was created from crepe paper in the form of a box, about four foot square and six feet high. Inside was a light that would be switched on, and the shimmering paper would look as if it were in flames. The play had been rehearsed and performed several times without incident. When the performance was nearly over and Leah Medley (portraying Leah Smock) entered the crepe-paper smoke house, the lamp was switched on, and the audience began screaming. The paper had caught fire! Many wondered if Leah Smock was the cause. It is hard to ignore that the name of both girls was Leah, and the only incident of this nature occurred at the Battletown School, perhaps on the old Smock property and within a half mile or so of Leah's grave.

There are more stories about the grave of Leah Smock. High school boys use to take their dates to the Betsy Daily Cemetery on Halloween. To some, it was a rite of passage. This story I firmly believe because I know the character of the man who told me. A group of students took their dates to the cemetery on one such Halloween. The witching hour of midnight had come and gone, and nothing happened. Being a November eve and chilly, the girls wanted to return to the cars, a long walk either way to get back; however, it's one way in and the same way out. The boys had flashlights and began walking toward the cars. They walked and walked, for what seemed to be a long enough time to get back, before one of the boys said, "I see something up ahead." The boys trained their lights on the object and found it was Leah's tombstone. They were back where they started. Shaken a little but undaunted, another boy said, "I'll lead us back." Once again, they walked for far longer than they needed to arrive at the cars and came right back to Leah's grave. This was repeated until nearly dawn, when they finally found their cars and went home. I have heard many variations on this story, and to be sure, some of them may have been helped along a little by alcohol. But this one wasn't. It's true and happened just this way.

One of the ladies at the old library warned me, "If you go to that cemetery, do not take any of the stones from Leah's grave." I told her that I had no intention of taking anything from her grave or the cemetery. She said to me in a hushed tone, "I know of one man who took a stone from Leah's grave and died soon afterwards."

Automobiles and off-road vehicles stall or their batteries go dead in the vicinity of the cemetery, and they must be pushed well away before they will start back up. Animals within the cemetery cannot be harmed and are almost tame. Two hunters hunting deer in the area spied a buck deer amongst the stones. While the deer was watching them, one of the men took aim and squeezed the trigger, but the rifle wouldn't fire. He tried again, and it still failed to function. He motioned for the other man to fire, but his gun also failed to fire. The deer simply stood unconcerned and watched the men. Finally, they walked back to their truck, and when they arrived there, their guns functioned flawlessly.

My friend Shirley Brown, the great-great-great-niece of Leah, is often called to give talks about her famous aunt. She was asked to do a special program at the Meade County Public Library in October 2012. She decided to write a short history of the event as an outline for the program. After writing the outline and narrative, Shirley began to print it from her computer. There has never before or since been a problem printing anything she has written. She edited the document and hit "file," "print," and "enter," and the printer began printing. The pictures of the grave printed in reverse. It was only legible by holding it up to a bright light and reading it through the backside of the paper. Leah seems to make herself known from time to time even through a computer.

I was typing this chapter and had written the last line when I saw at the bottom of the page a partial line of type that shouldn't have been there. I scrolled down, and as I read it, I found it was the first line of the chapter. Some way, I had typed the story in a circle and came right back to the same place I started. I thought to myself, "Oh, Leah." I had to print the pages and then delete and retype half of this chapter. I could hear her laughter.

Since writing the previous paragraph, another happening occurred that may have been influenced by Leah. On October 14, 2013, the Meade County Public Library was having an open house. It was a time for all of the various library programs and organizations affiliated with the library to showcase their organizations. Pamphlets were to be passed out from tables set up to accommodate each of the various clubs and programs. MCHAPS had a table, and Shirley Brown, a few days before the open house, was busily downloading photographs of various MCHAPS meetings onto a flash drive. She was going to set up her laptop computer to continuously display the photographs for potential members to see what happens at our meetings. All of the meetings that Shirley selected were downloaded without incident, until she tried to download the meeting where she made a presentation about Leah. That meeting could not be downloaded. After repeatedly trying, Shirley felt it was a glitch in the equipment and, therefore, went to another computer and e-mailed the photographs to her laptop, so she could complete the project that way. No matter what Shirley did, those photos of the Leah Smock presentation could not be downloaded.

Kay Hamilton and I wrote a story together for our local newspaper entitled "True Stories about the Witch's Grave." In it, we told some of the legendary tales. It was submitted by e-mail attachment along with photographs. We waited, but the story did not come out in print. One of the reporters phoned a couple of weeks later and asked when we would send in the piece and was surprised when I said we had done that. In some inexplicable way, it had gone into another computer file other than where it was sent. It was located in a computer file it never should have gone into and was finally published. Leah Smock seems to have a penchant for amusing herself with modern technology.

Not long ago, Mr. Eddie Price, who wrote a magnificent book entitled *Widder's Landing*, appeared at a book signing we arranged prior to our MCHAP meeting, where later Eddie addressed the society. We had set up some tables in the library when Beverly Furnival came over to the table where Shirley Brown and I were seated. She handed several typed pages to Shirley and said, "I wrote this for you." When Shirley completed reading it, she handed me the papers, and I saw it was a poem about Leah Smock. I asked Beverly and Shirley if they would honor me by allowing me to include the poem in this book. To my delight, they said yes.

Beverly wrote an introductory note to Shirley, and I include it here to explain some slight differences between the poem and what we have written.

> Shirley, you are the first person to see this poem. I used 'literary license,' in the poem using my imagination where we don't know what happened. The only thing I know isn't true is that Leah wasn't born in Battletown, but I think it makes the narrative line better.
>
> Hope you like it!
>
> Beverly

I am envious of Beverly. She can express in a few words what takes me dozens. The following poem is authored by Beverly Furnival:

"The Ballad of Leah Smock"

On a winter's night in Battletown
A baby girl was born.

The midwife gasped and removed the caul*
As the mother, faint, looked on.

Her Ma knew well the augury
And her little darling's fate.
For she herself had borne the caul
On her very own birth date.

The veil between the worlds was thin
That January night.
And little Leah Smock was doomed
To have the second sight.

CHORUS:
And, oh, the moon was full that night
And the wind was wicked strong.
And the embers rose and turned to stars
While the wind howled the devil's song.

The girl had hair as black as night
Her eyes were black as coal.
A slender build, endearing smile,
Quite lovely to behold!

As Leah grew, her mother taught
The lore of wood and flower,
The benefit of mallow root,
The tansy's secret power,

Infusions, tinctures, healing teas,
And poultices for pain;
But more than that: she loved to roam
In nature's sweet domain.

She knew the art of speaking with
The voles and squirrels and birds.
They seemed to understand her thoughts
When she beckoned without words.

And even frogs and snakes would fill
Her pure heart with delight.
But above them all was one true friend
Who had made her hours bright.

She met him once by yonder stream
And little did she know
That he'd become her constant guide,
And his name was Indian Joe.

Joe taught her much of Indian ways.
Of how to smell the air,
And know if rain or drought would come
Or winter snows were near.

A forking stick he cut for her
"A condon stick," he taught.
"Twill help you dowse a well, or find
What's lost when you cannot."

The stick she placed beside the hearth
But children came one morn,
And ran off crying "witching stick!"
That's how the "witch" was born.

CHORUS:
And, oh, the moon was full that night
And the wind was wicked strong.
And the embers rose and turned to stars
While the wind howled the devil's song.

Leah, it's true, could hold a babe
And oft make its fever fly.
Though often, too, she'd know full well
The little one would die.

But when she spoke and said the thing
She knew would soon occur,

The town folk grieved and soon declared
It was because of her!

One day she passed a farmer who
Had bought two comely Bays.
Somehow she knew by watching them,
They'd eaten tainted maize.

"Please let me touch your horses fine!"
She pleaded with the man.
She hoped to save them through the power
Of her often healing hand.

The farmer spat and pushed Leah down.
"No witch's spawn, I vow,
Will touch these bonny creatures that
I plan to put to plow."

Alas! The morrow's morn did find
Both horses stone-cold dead.
And cross the bottomlands of Meade
Leah's reputation spread.

CHORUS:
And, oh, the moon was full that night
And the wind was wicked strong.
And the embers rose and turned to stars
While the wind howled the devil's song.

One love she had a boy named Will
So loyal and so dear!
She'd healed him of consumption when
The end of life was near.

He loved her deep and true although
His preacher Pa proclaimed
"We shall not suffer a witch to live!"
In all things Leah was blamed.

The preacher riled the locals up;
Will tried to calm them down,
But naught could stop the hate that ran
Like fire through the town.

And that is how one moonlit night
Two brothers had a notion
To take their preacher's words to heart
With passionate devotion.

One armed himself with knives, one bore
A rope across his shoulder;
A bottle full of *lightening* served
To make the brothers bolder.

They made their way to the "witch's" home.
Poor Leah saw them coming.
And instantly she knew their hearts,
Her own heart fiercely drumming.

Quick to the drying shed she ran
And closed the door behind her.
No match was she for the brawny lads
Who pushed right in–to bind her.

Around her waist and wrists they wound
The rope and then they tied it.
They threw her down and locked the shed
With Leah Smock inside it.

As Leah struggled, drenched in fear,
She heard a fire crackle.
The shed soon filled with smoke and flame,
But she could not loose her shackle.

CHORUS:
And, oh, the moon was full that night
And the wind was wicked strong.

And the embers rose and turned to stars
While the wind howled the devil's song.

Her screams rose to the sky that night.
They went on and on and on.
By the time her Ma and Pa returned
From town, the shed was gone.

"Why did you not your powers use?"
Her mother bitterly cried.
"If you only had cast a spell.
Then you would not have died."

The town folk heard of the witch's death.
Her vengeful ghost they feared.
They piled her grave with boulders high
(Though many have disappeared).

They did not want to mark the grave
But Will, her beau, soon came
And in a slab of limestone carved
Her date of death and name.

For some strange reason 'round her grave
All hunters are disarmed.
The snakes curl up and sun themselves.
The squirrels are never harmed.

They say her ghost still haunts the woods
In a purple-colored mist.
She wears a long white dress, they say,
With black at waist and wrist.

So if you ever choose to go
And seek the graveyard out,
If the moon is full then chances are
Leah Smock might be about.

And if you do, I beseech of you
To leave the girl in peace.
Go home and pray, "Dear God, someday,
May fear and hatred cease."

CHORUS:
And if the moon is full that night
And the wind is wicked strong.
You'll see embers rise and turn to stars
While the wind howls the devil's song.

Beverly Furnival, 2012

*a piece of membrane that covers a newborn's head and face imme-diately after birth, often associated with psychic powers

Chapter 14

WAS LEAH A WITCH?

T he honest answer is no one knows. She has been called one since 1830, more or less, and there is anecdotal evidence that she could foretell the weather and predict or cause the deaths of people. She was very intelligent, excelled in her school work, and was at the top of her class. She had an abnormal way with animals, getting even those that were high-strung or mean to behave. She had a way with plants and could produce a fine garden. She carried a staff shaped like a serpent, and serpents, especially venomous ones, abound in the area in which she is buried. Some said she wore a rope belt around her waist. She was known to say her bedtime prayers, but "Cowboy" Bennett curiously stated that she worshipped the "old way." What did he mean by that? Her mother was described by some as a "powerful Kentucky witch" who taught Leah her craft. There is no doubt that Leah suffered bad press due to her odd habits of spending so much time in the woods and fields. She lashed out at those who refused to cater to her whims, be it to hold a baby or to pet a horse. She kept odd hours and seemed to be vengeful, yet she had girlfriends, a boyfriend, and Indian Joe with whom she associated, and she be-longed to a family who obviously loved her. She, like most country people, could read the signs of nature. Almanacs had been around for well over a hundred years, and if you knew the star and moon signs, you could regularly predict the seasons. She forecasted the deaths of many people, but one account says that most of them were critically ill, and predicting a critically-ill person in the 1830s would die was sure. The fact that she could tame animals is an interesting thing. She obviously studied them and knew their moods or fears from their actions. Domestic animals, such as dogs, that bite could well have only needed a kind hand to make them behave. There is a television show I have seen two or three times called *The Dog Whisperer* where bad dogs are made to behave by teaching the owners how to react to the actions of the animals. She well may have observed the animals enough to learn these things. She could grow plants like no other., and she knew their properties, like knowing that the root systems of poisonous plants could kill the cows that drank from the pond around which they grew. Perhaps she knew some of the old fertility charms or talked to her plants. Plants are living things, and they respond to kind treatment by growing larger and better. Some experiments show that plants respond favorably when soothing music is broadcast to the fields. She wore a rope around her waist, and her sleeves were tied at her wrists and neck. She carried a staff or rod. The rope or cords could have been a kind of cheap belt or garter, and the staff could have been a walking stick used like a cane. It is true that some medieval witches used riding poles before they substituted broomsticks, and it is reported that some used cords. There is a possibility here that she knew something of the old arts. She "worshipped in the old way" certainly could allude to the Old Religion, but it could also simply have meant the way Baptists worshipped when Squire Boone preached in this very area. Her mother was accused of being a witch, which might mean that Leah learned healing lore from her mother or that Leah and Margaret came from a line of hereditary witches. More likely was the possibility that the hysteria surrounding the Smock family simply spilled over from Leah to her mother. Her mother could have only been perceived as a witch. She spent hours in the woods and fields, and I think left school early because of her intelligence and being first in her class. She probably learned as much as the teacher could teach. She probably lashed out at people because she was an egocentric adolescent who was simply attempting to cope with the physical and emotional stresses going on within her. Most teenagers are difficult, but that didn't begin with our generation. She could have kept odd hours to watch the nocturnal animals and study their behavior or simply stayed up late and slept in. Maybe she watched the stars to determine the signs. Things like the cabin blowing down happened occasionally, and people often broke bones or suffered cuts and abrasions because their tools were almost all hand-employed. A thought comes to mind about people going crazy or losing their minds. In our culture, especially with the advent of air conditioning, television, and the like, more people stay indoors. As late as the 1950s and 1960s, sunstroke was a problem taken seriously. One of the early signs of sunstroke (medically defined as insolation or thermic fever)[102] was disorientation, followed by unconsciousness, and death. The people who became disoriented and blamed their condition on Leah's witching them may have suffered from exposure to the sun. In the case of the two children, they very well could have scared themselves into running away from Leah and then became lost, disoriented, and overheated. Of course, Leah could have said something to frighten them first. These incidents do not prove witchcraft, and more likely the perception of all of these things, combined with rumor and gossip, aggregated to do her in.

If Leah was a witch, what kind of magic or spells would she have adopted to cause her mischief in Lapland? Before we answer that question, we need to ask "does magic work?". One of my anthropology professors at the University of Louisville was Dr. Edwin Segal. At that time, he studied cultures on the African continent, which had less-sophisticated economic systems that some would describe as primitive. I sought his opinion about an African tribal mask I had, and he identified it as West African and genuine because of the homespun cloth, and the wormholes in the wood that attested to its age. He said the mask was probably used in making magic or in rituals of some type. For some reason, I asked him if magic worked. Ed answered, "Yes, magic works for those that practice it," and then he added, "In the same way prayer works for those that practice that." I found that to be a very satisfactory answer. It is interesting to me that those people who pray for something and it does not happen explain, "God said no." They might even say, "God said to wait for now," or "in God's good time." Because these people make allowances for prayers that do not seem to benefit them, their faith in prayer remains unchanged. And when the prayer is answered affirmatively, their faith is still unchanged. The people who claim to practice magic also make excuses, such as "I didn't do it correctly. It has to be repeated or "The time was not favorable." While all of these things are different, they are all similar in one respect: they answer the question of why it didn't work. Again their faith seems undaunted. Of course, when magic produced the desired effects, "The spell worked." Whether or not magic really works is not relevant in today's world because it is an anachronistic belief, "out of place in time." Magic is associated with animistic and polytheistic religions that exist or existed in cultures that have less complex economies than ours today. One would have to backtrack way beyond the Middle Ages to find a proper economy for that belief to fit. Of course, that does not dissuade many people from attempting to practice sorcery or from being superficially or pseudo-polytheistic. In many areas of the world, however, witchcraft and magic are still widely practiced.

Chapter 15
WHAT ARE CHARMS, SPELLS, AND MAGIC?

W itches are reputed to cast spells and make charms and talismans to effect supernatural intervention. We can never know with certainty what witchcraft Leah and Margaret engaged in, if any, but we can look at common medieval witch practices to determine what Leah and other witches might have practiced.

Charms, Spells, and Talismans

Charms that were made to be carried or worn can be generally divided into three classes: (1) Charms that are made in the form of rings, broaches, bracelets, bangles, etc., and that contain precious stones or natural objects, such as a rabbit's foot or four-leaf clover; (2) Charms that are engraved or chased with various designs; (3) Charms that are drawn on parchment or paper or even on the back of a mirror in the form of a square, circle, pentagram, hexagram, or any other form specifically designed to enclose or contain a power that will operate for the benefit of the wearer.[103] Certain stones were believed to bring good luck or be propitious for the wearer. Numbers are connected with the signs of the zodiac. The number two is associated with Virgo and Virgo to the precious stones pink jasper and hyacinth; therefore, by knowing zodiac signs and numbers and someone's date of birth, you will also know the corresponding precious stones for each sign. These stones would be incorporated in the ring, broach, or other ornament you wished to use as a charm. See the following chart:

Period in which the Sun is in the various signs of the Zodiac

Sign	Date Span	Number	Stone
Aries	March 21 to April 20	13	Diamond
Taurus	April 21 to May 22	14	Emerald
Gemini	May 23 to June 21	17	Agate
Cancer	June 22 to July 22	18	Ruby
Leo	July 23 to Aug. 22	19	Sardonyx
Virgo	Aug. 23 to Sept. 22	2	Sapphire
Libra	Sept. 23 to Oct. 22	3	Opal
Scorpio	Oct. 23 to Nov. 21	4	Topaz
Sagittarius	Nov. 22 to Dec. 22	7	Turquoise
Capricorn	Dec. 23 to Jan. 20	8	Garnet
Aquarius	Jan. 21 to Feb. 19	9	Amethyst
Pisces	Feb. 20 to March 20	12	Bloodstone[104]

Cornelius Agrippa, the 16th century adept and author of the classic work, *The Occult Philosophy*, gave the following list of signs and stones:

Sign	Stone
Aries	Sardonyx
Taurus	Carnelian
Gemini	Topaz
Cancer	Chalcedony
Leo	Jasper
Virgo	Emerald
Libra	Beryl
Scorpio	Amethyst
Sagittarius	Sapphire
Capricornus	Chrysoprase
Aquarius	Crystal
Pisces	Lapis-luzuli[105]

In addition to precious stones set in rings and other pieces of jewelry, there are charms made in differing shapes and designs. An anchor made of iron is an emblem of hope associated with the sea or water. A charm in the shape of a swallow, particularly in silver, is considered to be very lucky, as is an acorn, for youthfulness and vigor. Native American arrowheads and axes were carried to ward off evil intentions and are especially effective for Cancer and Sagittarius signs. Knots stand for the joining of things, and knots have long been used as symbols for lovers, i.e. when two people marry, they tie the knot. *Note: At a recent wedding I attended, a garland of flowers was wrapped around the couple's joined hands. This was done by the woman performing the marriage, harkening back to the old Celtic ceremony of hand fasting (the symbolic binding of the bride and groom together).* The owl is the sign for wisdom, and those that wish to gain knowledge can use it. Gold, silver, or copper are the best metals to use. Four-leaf clover and horseshoes are lucky, as is the left hind foot of a rabbit. Many of these things are in the realm of common superstition and certainly Leah could have known all of them. Leah was accused of harming her neighbors; therefore, let's look at spells she might have cast.

A spell is defined as: 1 a: a spoken word or form of words held to have magic power: b: a state of enchantment 2: a strong compelling influence or attraction.[106] So, we find a charm is an object to be carried or worn, and a spell is spoken, possesses magic power and will induce a state of enchantment on someone or something. Usually, spells were bound at the end of the recitation or other procedure with a rhyme. To curse an enemy, heal the sick, or aid a friend, the witch would make a poppet (doll). A relic from the subject of the spell, whether to heal or harm, was required: a hair, a drop of blood, a fingernail paring, a photograph, some clothing worn, or some other object containing their essence. Perhaps that essence of yesterday, in today's enlightened age, is D.N.A. The witch would carefully mold or model a character of the subject in wax or clay with the relic pushed into the material. It was not necessary that the poppet look exactly like the person for which it was intended. The idea was that whatever the witch did to the image would happen to the person. This harkens back 30,000 years to the caves of France, where the Cro-Magnon made images of animals and then put arrows in them in order to ensure success in the upcoming hunts. If you subject the image to curative herbs and beneficial medicine, the person should get better; conversely, if something negative is done to the image, that negativity would be visited on the person in whose image it was made.

An old spell to protect against one who would do one harm involved the witch lighting three candles in a triangle and writing the name of the person to be protected from on a piece of paper three times, crossing out the name each time before it was written again. The paper was burned and the ashes placed in a box. The candles were blown out counter-clockwise, and the box was buried at a crossroads. A stick was shoved in the ground and broken, with the broken portion pointing in the direction of the subject's home.

To punish a person who has done harm, a hazel switch cut on Good Friday night was used to whip an enemy, no matter where he or she might be. The witch would simply lash the switch about in their home, and no matter how far away the enemy, it is believed he or she would feel the lashing. Hazel is a most useful bush or tree. It was thought hazel pins driven into the beams of houses protected them from fires, and a hazel wand or walking stick cut on Walpurgis Night is said to protect from stumbling in the dark.

The witch would write on a piece of paper or parchment "Whomever this charm shall wear no man may take, no man may snare. Unscathed shall he stay till have passed a year and a day!" Again the spell would be bound with a rhyme, either one previously written or one made up on the spot. There was believed to be something strange about rhyme. After making an invocation or casting a spell, the spell was bound with a rhyme, such as:

> Let it be done by thy decree,
> Begin the ancient Law of Three![107]

Another such rhyme supposed to be especially effective in love spells was "Delightful sport whose never-ending charm makes young blood tingle and old blood warm."

In reading some of the old charms and spells of the medieval witches, some curious things are noted. Witch binding rhymes and rhyming charms are very nearly like children's nursery rhymes: "Eeny meny, miney, mo, catch a tiger by his toe, if he hollers let him go, eeny, meny, miney, mo," is a variation on a children's rhyme used on the playground to choose sides in a game or to see who's first at bat. It is very much like the medieval rhyme for a spell "Any, meny, mona, my, Barcalony, stony, sty, harum, scarum, frownum, ack, harrieum, barrieum, wi, wi, wo, whack!" Some medieval chants have persisted until the present day in the form of Mother Goose Rhymes and likely their true meanings are long forgotten. So it is in the dancing game "Ring around the Rosie," which I guess we have all played as a child. Its meaning has been obscured but can still be found and has to do with the Black Plague.

By 1347, the Bubonic or Black Plague had devastated Eurasia and descended on Europe. The plague brought into being a new form of treating the dead. It was thought that the disease would continue to remain alive in the bodies and that the dead may well rise from the grave in the form of vampires or other creatures undead, re-infecting the population. For this reason, the bodies of those who died from the plague were cremated. People who died in ordinary ways were buried as usual in the church yard. Some way for the "body carts" (wagons used by undertakers) was needed to differentiate between plague victims and others so that the bodies could be treated appropriately. The nursery rhyme was born out of the manner decided upon to indicate plague victims, the symptoms of the disease, and the treatment of the body after death.

Bubonic plague was noted by red spots on the face and body; each spot was called a rosy. As the disease worsened, a ring formed around the red spot, foretelling that the patient would soon die. To let the undertakers know who was a plague victim, some person lost to memory came up with putting posies (common flowers) in the pockets of the people killed by the plague. The bodies so identified were burned. Thus we have the nursery rhyme:

> Ring around the rosy
> A pocket full of posies
> Ashes, ashes,
> All fall down

For any who have never played this game as children, the girls and boys join hands in a circle or ring and dance clockwise, right to left, around the circle chanting the rhyme. When the words "All fall down" are spoken, the children all fall down. I haven't played the game in more than sixty years, but I remember it as a child being great fun. It is, however, also an example of how the chants and dances from the Middle Ages can last far into the future where the meanings are often forgotten.

It is interesting to me that the observations and cycles of nature, when used to predict what the weather will be or the growth of crops, appears as if there is some kind of magical or mystical divination occurring. That was not so then and not so today. A few people know some of these things while most are ignorant of them. Old people knew more about nature, and in our modern society where we have sophisticated technology and specialists like meteorologists whom we depend on, the old ways are supplanted and forgotten. I once learned of an Indian method of predicting how much daylight was remaining in a day. I learned this in the Boy Scouts when I was about twelve years old. This method used by early pioneers and Native Americans has served me well, especially when I am on an evening hunt. This method can prove very helpful if you have a long way to walk from where you are hunting to get back to the place where you parked—say a half hour's walk away—or if you're in an area with which you are unfamiliar. The afternoon sun will be low in the sky and above the horizon of the treetops. This is easy to discern when on the ground with a clear view of the sky. Hold up your right hand, with the palm facing you, and put the bottom of your little finger touching the top of the treetop horizon. The bottom of the sun will be higher or lower than your first finger. But for the sake of this exercise, if the bottom of the sun sits on top of your first finger when your little finger is on the top of the tree line, you now have about one hour of daylight left in which to hunt or make your way back to the car. You could hunt for a half an hour and walk back, getting to your car about dark, or hunt for an hour and walk back in the dark. Each finger width below the sun equals approximately fifteen minutes of daylight. There is nothing magical about this, but it has impressed some of the people with whom I have hunted. I tell them how long it will be before it will be dark, and I don't have to use my watch. I simply hold up my hand and accurately estimate the amount of daylight remaining.

There is a book, *Living Magic* by Ronald Rose, that describes a technique the Australian Bushmen used when traveling long distances. It is sort of a mental hypnotism that seems to allow them to travel great distances more quickly. The Apache and Yuma Indians practiced something similar. Dr. J. B. Rhine, when he was the Director of the Parapsychology Laboratory at Duke University, wrote the foreword to Ronald Rose's book. In it, Rose describes ways the Aborigines travel quickly from place to place with uncanny speed.

Rose wrote, "At a place called Pretty Gully there was a woman named Lillie Dunn who was sick and some thought she was near death. 'Her people rang up Tabulam Station [about ten miles distant] and asked him to send out the old fellow that cured me because they thought Lillie Dunn would die. They said he would come out in no time, and sure enough he did.'

"How long did it take him?"

"He was there in a flash."

"An hour?"

"No, less than that."

"Half an hour?"

"No. No time."

"A quarter hour?"

"No. No time."

"Five minutes?"

No, just a minute."[108]

The bush doctor arrived on the scene just a minute after he was summoned. How could this have happened? The Australian Aborigines practiced a type of thought travel and hypnotism that was said to allow them to travel great distances quickly. A man named Major was said to do this. "This fellow's name was Major," said Harry. He used to work on the cane fields with us. Every Saturday when we knocked off work, me and my mates would go straightaway into the town, about four miles away. When we would get there, Major would always be there before us. Sometimes, he left after us. No matter how fast we went, he always got there first. We said to that fellow, "How do you get here so quick?" and he said, 'I got clever things and they carry me here.'[109] Similarly, coastal natives believed in this ability to travel fast that so closely resembles the claims of the Yogi of Tibet. There is evidence, too, that, in a sort of trance state, a native might become aware of events at a distance as though he had clairvoyance. Geronimo the Apache war chief had this. Technically, this is known as "traveling clairvoyance." There is no doubt that natives believe they actually experience this.[110] Other Native Americans had this ability, as well.

One noted incidence of this occurred in Walker, Minnesota in the 1890s. My grandfather Arthur Clarence Bryant and his older brother, Mathias Marmaduke Bryant, were boys. Their father, William Walter Bryant, was an important homesteader in the area of the town of Walker in Cass County, Minnesota. This event was one of many that led to the last official Indian War in the United States in October 1898.

The Ojibwa Indians occupied the area across Leech Lake and north of Walker. They had been abused by the local timber barons, sheriffs, and marshals in the area and were angry. We always called Uncle Mathias Marmaduke "Uncle M. M." for obvious reasons. One day, William Walter had to go into town on business and took his two sons, Arthur and Mathias. The boys wandered off to explore the town and window shop. Now at that time, there were lots of Native Americans in the area. Walker had a population of about two hundred whites and there were an estimated twenty thousand Indians in the same locale. The Indian men, by custom, would not acknowledge a woman or child they passed on the road. They would, however, acknowledge a white man by holding up a hand, palm outward, as if to say, "hello or hi there." Arthur was younger than Mathias by some three years. While they were on the street, the boys saw a group of four or five town bullies about their own age beating up a single Indian boy. Mathias lit into the fight on the side of the Indian, and the two of them soon whipped and chased off the white bullies. Arthur, my grandfather, said that the streets were empty, and no one was evident that could have seen the fight. Soon after the fight, the streets teemed with Indian men and women. Although there was no way in that short span of time for them to have seen or been told of what happened, they all seemed to know. Uncle M. M. was only fourteen years old, but from that day and forevermore, when Indian men met him on the street or road, they acknowledged him by raising their hands. This may have been a case of traveling clairvoyance.[111]

When these people wish to fast travel, they do a sort of self-induced hypnosis and travel in stages by visualizing where they will be, concentrating on that place, and seeing themselves there or beyond. Then, they visualize the next leg of the journey and visualize being at that place and so forth. After a while, they begin to "fast travel"—travel great distances in a short period of time.

I will relate one other thing some would call magic while others would call it a natural occurrence. There was an anthropology student at the University of Louisville who shared a class with me and showed me this. This student was sitting on the ground, intent on staring at the sky. It was a bright and breezy fall day, and the clouds were light and fluffy. I asked what she was doing, and she told me making clouds disappear. She told me to sit on the ground and look at the sky. Pick out a fluffy cloud, not a really big one, but one you like. Stare at the cloud while you concentrate on its breaking up and disintegrating. And, in just a matter of minutes, it will. I did, and it did. Is this magic, or just the nature of fluffy white clouds? It is the natural tendencies of clouds to form, dissolve, and reform, but we almost never closely observe clouds.

Could Leah have discovered these things and used the techniques to either amuse herself or impress the locals or to make the distances she wandered away from home at night seem less far? Perhaps she did. Lastly, what about intuition and clairvoyance? We know that there are people that make predictions that come true. We also know that some people seem to know what others are thinking. People like Jeanne Dixon seemed to be able to foretell the future. I really don't know if any of that is true, but I can relate one incident that might seem to suggest that possibility. During the 1960s, Dr. J. B. Rhine at Duke University's Parapsychology Department created a deck of cards and did some clinical testing on subjects to see if there was evidence indicating the ability to read the tester's mind or foretell their order. A deck of twenty-five cards was developed that had five cards in a suit and five suits. The suits were simply five geometric shapes, one on each of the cards in a suit. The suits were a square, a circle, several wavy lines, a five pointed star, and a triangle. The law of averages states that any one subject guessing what card is being held up by the person testing, without the tester disclosing the image to the subject, will get five correct answers. This is interpreted to mean that anyone who consistently gets more than five correct guesses has some innate ability of E.S.P. above the average person. Conversely, anyone that consistently gets less than five correct hits shows an abnormality in the other direction. During the 1960s, the Louisville Society for Psychical Research that was conducting ESP experiments formed and operated for three or four years at the Louisville Free Public Library at 3rd and York Streets in Louisville, Kentucky. The object of the society was to determine if any subjects or experiences investigated proved psychical events or that E. S. P. existed. While this group tested dozens of people, perhaps a hundred or more, there was only one case that really seemed striking. Lots of people would get more than five hits on a test run of twenty-five, but after twenty-five test runs, their average would remain right at twenty-five, slightly more or less. This did not really indicate any extra sensory perception.

One Saturday afternoon at the Louisville Free Public Library, the society had a speaker from the Louisville Police Department, Detective

Chester Dettweiler, formerly of the bunko and fraud section of L. P. D., but he was then doing public relations. A complaint had been received about a "fortune teller" who was preying on gullible and fearful people for the purpose of fraudulently acquiring their money. One elderly lady had already shelled out hundreds of dollars because the fortune teller would end her sessions by telling her that she must come back to avoid some calamity or another. She would do this and pay many more of her pension dollars to the fortune teller, always with the same admonition to come back. The society acquired what information it could and turned that information over to the police. (After a visit from the "bunko squad," the fortune teller ceased her scam.) The society asked for someone knowledgeable about the law to address what the law was regarding such activities. Thus, the officer came and addressed the society. After his talk was completed, tables were set up for the testing of people for E. S. P. Because of the interest in the speaker, there were many new people there, who had not previously been tested.

The testing was done at different tables around the room. A sheet of paper was given for the person being tested to fill out general information of name, address, and telephone number. That information was necessary to mail out a newsletter. On the reverse side of the paper, there were two columns of twenty-five lines, numbered one through twenty-five consecutively. The subject and the tester sat across from each other. The suits were shown to the subject, and the testing began by the cards being thoroughly shuffled. The deck was placed in front of the tester, and a card was lifted from the top. The subject was given ten seconds to blindly determine what the suit of that card happened to be. The tester wrote in the left column what the card actually was and in the right column what the subject guessed. The papers were stacked to be later scored when the meeting was over. A tall, lean young man was there and wanted to be tested. He was given a paper and told to sit down at the table, and one of the ladies testing took a seat across from him. Because there were only a few testers and lots who wanted to be tested, the testers were backed up in a hurry. He handed her his paper, and she immediately began the testing process. He missed every guess. She placed a check mark on that sheet to indicate it was an abnormality and needed to be examined. She then moved on to test the next subject. Later when the abnormalities were checked, it was found that this young man, except for the first guess, exactly predicted the next card to be turned up. Turning his sheet over to get his information and tell him the results, it was found to have been left blank. He was never seen again at the meetings, and no one knew who he was. To my knowledge, his was the only example reported by the L.S.P.R. that seemed to indicate the presence of E.S.P. Of course, although I think unlikely, it could have been a fluke.

Intuition is a reality. Some people just know when a visit is about to occur or something is about to happen. When my mom's nose itched, she would say company's coming. Many times it did. Shirley Brown said if her mother dropped a spoon, she would say a woman is coming to visit; conversely, if she dropped a fork, it was a man who would drop by. My mother and father could sit at a table, and they were so tuned in to each other, they conversed in short sets of seemingly unconnected words, and each knew what the other was thinking. It used to drive me nuts. Was this E. S. P.? No, it wasn't, but it could be construed to be. I found it particularly frustrating at Christmas time, when they were thinking and sort of talking about gifts.

Both of my grandmothers and my mother believed that things happened in threes. If there was an engagement, marriage, accident, or death, they would say that soon there would be two more. All three of them took great pride in pointing out the fact that three of whatever incident finally occurred. While this run of three did not happen every time, it did seem to happen more often than not. These things fall into the realm of superstitions.

Superstitions and Witchcraft

Leah probably knew such things and was superstitious, which may explain why Leah was thought to be a witch. Perception can be considered factual, even when it isn't. For example, Daniel Boone was known to be a great Indian fighter who killed many Indians; however, when he was interviewed by a reporter late in his life, he was asked how many Indians he had killed. He said that he knew he had killed three Indians but acknowledged that he had shot some more. This admission flies in the face of how he is perceived. In the same way, it would be interesting to ask some questions about Leah. How many predictions did she make that didn't come true? I bet there were some. Could the man who sold the horses to the Lapland farmer know something was wrong with them, and that's why he sold them? Maybe the baby she was said to bewitch died from pre-existing illness, and Leah was trying to help. The hurtful adolescent behavior saying "you'll be sorry" to the parents when not allowed to hold the baby was probably just a mean thing for a teen to say. And the fact that she came back to see the baby after it died does not seem to me the action of a killer, just the opposite. If anything, it shows she cared about the child, wanting to see it one more time. The animals howling or on the roof could be related or unrelated to Leah, or if Leah was a witch or lycanthropic, perhaps she did cause that animal activity. Couldn't it be the animal behavior was in response to the grief of the parents and the death of the child or that they were sympathetic to Leah's grieving?

Chapter 16
A RECENT WITCHCRAFT TRIAL

In 1969, Arthur H. Lewis, a well-known author and former reporter, wrote a book entitled *Hex*. His book was a historical account of a November 28, 1929 murder in a sparsely-settled area of York County, Pennsylvania. The murder was committed at one minute past midnight by a practicing faith healer or powwow man also called a witch. John H. Blymire murdered another known witch and healer who Blymire believed had cast a spell over him. The witch who Blymire believed cursed him was Nelson D. Rehmeyer, a farmer in the North Hopewell Township, about four miles west of Shrewsbury. The murder was committed while trying to obtain Rehmeyer's witch book or a lock of his hair. William Bolitho, the *New York World's* noted correspondent wrote…only an hour, as the motor runs, from Philadelphia, genuine witches are killing each other at midnight with incantations and funeral fires. "Here at any rate, is antiquity as old and genuine and romantic as anything in Europe….Witchcraft and uncommonly orthodox witchcraft, is being practiced in blood and death only two blocks off Main Street by adepts in the pure tradition of terror and imagination of the stone age"…One introverted, intuitive farmer has made an attack on the subconscious mind of the other and has been attacked in return because "The only way to escape from ultimate destruction by this is to kill and bury his enemy symbolically by cutting off a lock of his hair and burying it eight feet deep….With two friends and fellow sufferers he attempts to accomplish this. The other wizard resists, is killed; his body burnt to make a ceremonial job of it."[112]

Blymire believed he had been hexed for many years. At one time in his life, he had been a powerful healer and witch, but after working for Rehmeyer many years earlier, he had suffered reversals in health

166

and stature, amongst others of his kind. For years, he sought out the help of those witches who could ward off evil spells or make charms or talismans of protection. After many years, his tormentor was pointed out and a means to stop the curse was given to him. The only way to escape from the ultimate destruction by this curse was to kill and bury his enemy symbolically.

"The funeral of the victim of the fiendish crime was held at two o'clock yesterday afternoon," reported the Hanover (Pennsylvania) *Record Herald* of December 3, 1928. "Following brief services at the funeral home of John T. Wagoner at Shrewsbury, the body was taken to St. John Sadler's Church in Hopewell Township where concluding services were held." Borne by six neighbors, the mortal remains of Nelson D. Rehmeyer were carried to the church cemetery on a hill beside the church, where they found a last resting place.[113]

When Blymire was told that a man he had worked for many years ago and whom he knew was the one who had hexed him and caused him so much pain throughout his life, he decided that he would steal Rehmeyer's witch book or get a lock of his hair, either of which would allow him to break the spell. Blymire and all the other witches in that area (including Rehmeyer) used a book written by John George Homan, entitled *The Long Lost Friend*. Homan wrote his book in 1805 (when Margaret Smock was about nine years old, being born in the same state), and in it was included pharmacopoeia and methodology for future generations. Homan claimed he was no hexer. He announced in 1816, "When you buy a book from Homan, you never receive a hex book." Lewis states that is as self-deluding a proclamation as can be imagined.[114]

When I look at the dates that overlap with the time that Margaret Smock lived in Pennsylvania and when John Smock was in New Jersey not that far away, it is reasonable to expect that either or both may well have had their own copy or copies of Homan's witch book, *The Long Lost Friend*. When Homan advertised his book in 1816, Margaret would have been about twenty years old.

When John Blymire was sixteen, not unlike Apache medicine men, he could cure the bite of the most venomous serpents, notably copperheads and rattlesnakes. He did so by touching the bite with his fingertips and making the sign of the cross three times and muttering the following verse:

God has created all things and they were good;
Thou only, serpent, art damned.
Cursed be thou and thy sting.
Zing, zing, zing.[115]

As time went on, he became a powwow man. Blymire was seventeen years old in 1912, but by 1920, he had been hexed to the point that he had sought the help of a score or more of the most powerful witches in the area. John Blymire knew of a March 24, 1924 murder when Sallie Jane Heagy shot her husband Erwin Samuel Heagy while he lay in bed at their home. Sallie was advised by a witch named Lenhart that her husband had hexed her, and she had to do something about him if she wanted to get better. The thing she did was shoot him to death. There was no doubt that John Blymire knew that a violent end could happen.

On July 10, 1928, less than five months before the Rehmeyer killing, Mrs. Helen Eiker of Gettysburg, Pennsylvania, shot and killed her husband Percy Eiker. She told the police that Percy had hexed her, and this was her way out. She, too, was advised by the witch Lenhart.

I do not know if Sallie and Helen really thought they were hexed–they may have just wanted to be done with trifling husbands, but that was their defense.

John Blymire was reminded that he had worked for Rehmeyer when he was younger. He was now thirty-two years old. He was told that Rehmeyer was the one who had hexed him. He then enlisted the aid of two accomplices to go to Rehmeyer's house and get a lock of his hair or to get his witch book. Wilbert Hess and John Curry joined Blymire in the second and fatal trip to Nelson D. Rehmeyer's farm. John Curry was about fourteen when he met John Blymire, and he looked up to the older man. Eighteen-year-old Wilbert Hess was the son of Milton Hess, with whom John Blymire was acquainted. Milton Hess was also a healer, and he approved of the plan Blymire had to break the spell. On the first visit, Blymire and company were unable to complete the task of locating the book, and Rehmeyer went upstairs to bed while the others slept downstairs in the kitchen. In the morning, they left, to return the following night with some lengths of heavy rope. They finally attacked Rehmeyer, a large, strong man. Rehmeyer was fighting very hard when they attempted to tie him, so one of the boys got a stick of stove wood and beat him to death. They then wrapped him in a blanket, set it on fire, searched the house, stole $2.80 in change, and made their escape. A short while later, they were caught.

Judge Ray Sherwood presided over the trial, and John Blymire was the first to be tried on January 8, 1929. The defense of Blymire was insanity because of a lifelong association with witchcraft. On January 9, John Blymire took the stand in his own defense. After testimony and a strong, almost pleading closing statement, the judge charged the jury, and they retired to their chamber at 5:40 p.m. At 7:30 p.m., the jury indicated that they had reached a verdict, and John Blymire was found guilty of first degree murder and sentenced to life imprisonment.

John Curry was the next to be tried, and he had what was probably the speediest trial on record for a charge this serious. His trial began at 9:30 a.m., and it was over at 4:00 p.m. when the defense rested. Court reconvened the next morning at 9:30 a.m., and by 10:50 on that morning of January 11, John Curry was found guilty of murder in the first degree and sentenced to life in prison. Wilbert Hess was found guilty of second degree murder and was given a sentence of ten to twenty years in prison. Thus, the Pennsylvania witchcraft trial of 1929 ended.

Could it happen again? It is unlikely, but anything is possible. When people are afraid, they take measures to protect themselves. Fear of things unseen and of a supernatural nature are fears primeval. An old saying is that you fight fire with fire. In Nelson D. Rehmeyer's case, whether he was guilty of hexing John Blymire or not, Blymire had the perception that he, Rehmeyer, did in fact cast a spell over him. To give himself relief from this degradation of his physical being, his life, and fortune, he lashed out in kind, killing a man in the process. There is little difference in the mindset of those who killed Leah Smock. Rightly or wrongly, she was accused of causing crops to fail and babies and farm animals to die and bewitching people near her home. Those people responded by not suffering a witch to live and burned her to death. It is interesting that, although these events were separated by eighty-eight years, they both occurred in rural areas where faith healing, herbalists, and superstitions were part of everyday life.

The Last Known Execution of a Witch by Burning

Leah Smock was not the last woman burned as a witch, although she was the younger of the two. Some fifty-five years after Leah was burned, another woman suffered the same fate. In 1877, Bridget Boland married Michael Cleary. He was a cooper, and she was a dress maker apprentice. Bridget was seventeen years old and Michael was twenty-six. The couple lived apart for several years: he built barrels in Clonmel, and she took care of her parents, made dresses, and tended her flock of geese and chickens. Bridget was an independent woman who often took long walks by herself and visited the fairy ringforts and their ruins remaining in this medieval area of Ireland. Michael later joined Bridget at her home in Tipperary, Ireland, and they searched about for a house of their own. The one they had selected had the reputation of being built on the site of a fairy ring or fort, making it less desirable but more affordable. Superstitious people were afraid of the little people, fairies, and witches but Bridget was not.

In March 1895, the winter in Ireland was one of the coldest on record, and twenty-six-year-old Bridget took ill. A doctor was sent for but didn't arrive for a week or more, and Michael visited a fairy doctor, a folk healer who prescribed medicinal herbs. When the treatments didn't help, Michael became convinced that the fairies had taken Bridget and replaced her with a changeling lookalike. His view was reinforced when a relative noticed that Bridget was unlike her former self. As she grew weaker, a priest was called, and she was given last rites. Sometime later, relatives visited Bridget and found an exorcism underway. The villagers were chanting and performing rituals while she was force fed herbs and milk. They threw urine on her because that was considered a good way to get rid of fairies. When these things didn't work, they held her over the hearth fire and prodded her with red-hot pokers to force out the demon possessing her. She was asked again and again if she was a fairy. Sometime after St. Patrick's Day, Bridget was reported missing. Michael claimed she was taken by the fairies, but her body was found in a shallow grave on March 22. The coroner's report declared she had died by burning. It was suspected she burned in the fireplace.

Michael Cleary was charged with murder, as were ten others. The legal hearings began April 1ˢ, 1895, and he was found guilty of manslaughter, sentenced to fifteen years in prison, and released April 28, 1910. This case has been called the last witch burning in Ireland and gave rise to a nursery rhyme "Are you a witch or are you a fairy? Or are you the wife of Michael Cleary?"

Chapter 17
Traditions Associated with Witchcraft

There are a number of things, other than healing and foretelling the weather, that witches are supposed to know about. One of the skills the witch was supposed to be proficient in was crystal gazing or "skrying." During the medieval period, owning glass was an expensive proposition reserved for the royal and very rich. To have a mirror or a sphere of glass or rock crystal was beyond the reach of the peasant class, from which most of the "wise ones" came. Therefore, some other medium had to be used to focus the seer's attention in an effort to answer questions about the future, and possession of a crystal could be evidence of sorcery. For these reasons, the Old Ones used a black iron pot or some other very dark or blackened vessel into which they poured clear water. This formed a black mirror to gaze into. While the L. S. P. R. was testing, subjects was limited to volunteers wanting to be tested. No evidence was ever found of anyone who could foretell events beyond one possible example, but it is possible Leah could have known about his practice. Other methods of foretelling events could have been used by Leah. One such method is the use of a pendulum or a dowsing rod. In the case of a pendulum, an object is suspended from a chain or sting, and a question is posed. The pendulum swings side to side or toward and away from the body, one direction for yes and the other for no. The pendulum is believed to swing by neural-idiom impulses supposedly innate within the user's body. I guess the question of "which direction indicates yes and which direction is no" arises. This method was used before ultrasound to determine the sex of babies prior to birth and to find lost objects. Shirley Brown used it to narrow down her search for a lost object by asking about various rooms where the lost item might be found. This type of foretelling or answering questions about the unknown is akin to dowsing.

Dowsing is the locating of something underground and hidden from view. There are too many stories of success by this method for me to personally doubt that it works. I have a good friend whose father dowsed to find underground water for wells and such. He used a forked slippery elm branch he gripped so tightly that the force pulling it down when he was above water would literally strip the bark from the branch. One example that was legendary at the Louisville Water Company, where I worked for a number of years while attending night school, was an aged man in the maintenance department on Almond Ave. who could dowse. He was only called out when all other means to find an underground water main leak had failed. Stethoscopes, probing, and other means were employed to locate main breaks. But when they failed, an old friend and associate, Carl Meyer, told me this fellow would take two pieces of copper wire, bend them into ninety degree angles, and ride out to the location of the pressure drop. He would then walk along the water main with a wire in each hand, and when he got over the leak, four feet below ground, the wires would cross. I am told that the backhoe would be sent out and that this old fellow in overalls would be accurate every time. Leah and Margaret may well have dowsed and used a pendulum.

There are to be sure other methods of divination, such as palmistry and card and tea leaf reading. Many people have shown faith in these techniques and either practice them or go to those that do. I have read of a Native American process to answer "yes or no" questions using three smooth stones of three different colors. This method of divination is entitled lithomancy. There was a very dark or black stone, a very light or white stone, and a neutral gray or beige indicator stone. A question requiring a yes or no answer was asked of a holy man, and he would remove the stones from a leather pouch and cast them onto a buffalo hide in front of him. The black stone meant a no, and the white stone meant a yes. If the indicator stone was closer to the white stone, the answer was yes; if it was closer to the black stone, the answer was no. If it were directly in between, the answer was unclear, and the stones were cast two more times. The idea was to get a consensus of three throws in the event of a first throw that was inconclusive. The technique is different than that of the pendulum or dowsing because the stones leave the practitioners' hands. If Leah had learned from Native Americans, i.e. Indian Joe, this type of divination may have been practiced by her.

Lycanthropy was associated with witchcraft in Western Europe and in Native American mythology. Today, it's more often associated with vampires and werewolves in the movies. Lycanthropy is the ability for a witch to change shapes and become an animal. In the case of a werewolf, the animal the person changed into was a wolf, while the vampire turned into a bat. European witches were supposed to have this power or ability, as did some Indian medicine men. There is one historic example of this in 1898 when the Ojibwa medicine man Bug-o-ney-ge-shig was said to watch the battle on Bear Island in Leech Lake between the United States Army and Ojibwa warriors. The holy man was said to have turned himself into a crow and watched the battle from his position high in a tree. Historians say he fled to Canada, but the Ojibwas' faith was so great at that late date they believed him.

The wearing of the head and horns of the animal in the old dances likely gave rise to the notion of lycanthropy. On a moonlit night, someone watching from afar might see a man or woman go into the brush and see a stag deer or goat emerge and join the dance, changed from human form to that of an animal. In that way, witches became known as skin-changers, shapeshifters, or lycanthropic.

Chapter 18
TOOLS OF THE TRADE

There are a number of tools witches are said to have used. The herbalists used a short, white-handled knife with a curved blade, sickle-shaped with the inside of the curve sharpened. This knife, called a "baleen," was traditionally used to procure herbs from the fields and forests. The blade shape made it easy to clip plants or bark from limbs or even twigs and small limbs from trees. The curved blade was also handy for digging and cutting sections from roots.

The wand, walking stick, or riding pole was also known as a condon. Some of these poles or wands were highly decorated with carved figures or designs. There is no doubt in my mind that some of the poles were cut from trees entwined by vines, which gave them a serpentine shape. Serpents were often subjects depicted by Native Americans and pioneers. The condon sticks were known to be used in fertility rituals intended to make the crops grow high. Of course, there could have also been other uses for them that are now long forgotten. Modern examples are to be found in magic shows, little black sticks white on one end that are used by illusionists, and of course the wands used by fairy godmothers and good witches like Glenda in *The Wizard of Oz*.

Cords are something witches used in working magic. The cords were said to be tied in places on their bodies where they would restrict the blood flow, causing a trance-like condition to occur. This could be a link to the Leah Smock legend. Cords have been prominently mentioned around her wrists and neck, as well as a rope at her waist. These cords seen on her apparition could, of course, be those with which her captors bound her.

Pentacles were also said to be used by witches. These were metal geometrically-shaped discs, carved with symbols in various forms and used in casting spells. According to lore, during the Inquisition, the pentacles were often made of wax so that they could be easily melted or so that the signs and symbols could be rubbed off them, eliminating evidence of sorcery.

Witches were also supposed to use an anthame, a black-handled knife for making instruments, such as the Condon stick, or carving the symbols into the pentacles. It was also said this double-edged knife, somewhat dagger-shaped, was used to call forth spirits, draw a circle around the practitioner, and perform other tasks of that nature.

Smoke from herbs or burning incense, as well as candles, was employed in the rituals to represent fire and air, and salt and water were also placed nearby to complete the four elements. A bowl or pot was used for burning incense, some of which could have been hallucinogenic. I think it is interesting to note that all of these things could take the shape of ordinary, everyday kitchen items, with the exception of the condon, for which the broomstick eventually substituted. The tools of the medieval witch and the peasant housewife were essentially the same. Miscellaneous items, such as jars, bottles, bowls, mortars and pestles, were found with both and are in almost every household today. There were other things that were said to be identifiable as witch-related. These things took the form of furniture or other everyday items that were deliberately made in an imperfect manner. For example, a three-legged stool that was common in most peasant houses would have two legs turned on a lathe or hand-carved with the spiral curves going up the legs, and the third leg being carved the other way with the curve being reversed. Things might be almost but not quite symmetrical or in some other way almost unnoticeable to everyday people and considered defective if noticed but would be identifiable to witches as having power.

What about the people who claim to be practicing witchcraft today? There are indeed modern witches or those that call themselves the same. They don elaborate robes or dress for their rituals in the East Indian tradition of being "sky clad" (nude). Some of them use black mirrors or tarot cards to make readings. It is my belief most of these folks are inoffensive people either looking for attention or fearful of the future and trying to exert control over their own lives or the lives of others. Control seems to be a motivating factor, causing a good many people to try to discern the future. Sometimes they exhibit paranoia. In fact, if we harken back to the Blymire story, his entire reason for killing Rehymeyer may have been because of the former's paranoia. His insanity defense was likely due to his paranoia and psychosis. It is interesting to me that Blymire and his associates, one of whom had a father who was a witch, chose, when it got down to brass tacks, to beat a man to death with a stick of stove wood instead of using supernatural powers. Leah, to her mother's seeming surprise, was also unable to save herself. That seems to belie any magical power or ability and cast doubt over the efficacy of her magic.

There was another trait witches were supposed to exhibit—that of owning or having a familiar. The familiar was purportedly an animal that did the witch's bidding. It could be most any animal, but owls, bats, toads, dogs, and cats seemed to be the most common. These animals were said to be given oral directions by the witch and would do her bidding by delivering messages and returning them. The familiars were said to be gifts provided to the witch by the Devil. The traditional witch familiar in the shape of a cat was not black but rather fawn brindle. The subject of familiars is important, not for any magical reason, but rather for what they likely were and the damage I think they caused.

Most women accused of witchcraft were elderly and made their living by servicing their community with medicine and advice about the weather. Some advised in personal matters because of the wisdom they gained with age. In the natural course of things, the women of every era seem to outlive their male counterparts. Older women, often living alone, might keep a pet for company or protection. A bird, such as a crow, raven, or even an owl, might make a good, although unusual, pet. A dog, cat, goat, pig, cow, donkey, or horse might be owned by the witch. No matter what animal was owned, isn't it to be expected that she might talk to her animal friend? I know lots of people who talk to their pets. I suspect the love of a pet or the cursing of an obstinate donkey caused a good many medieval women to be burned. Any pet or livestock could be considered evidence of having a familiar. While in life Leah is not accused of having a familiar, there is ample evidence that she showed an affinity for animals of all types. She was said to have called up the animals to chase the boys who mistreated her. It was believed that the cats on the roof of the dead child's house were howling because of her. This, in my mind, added weight to the community belief she was a witch. Could she have changed herself into the copperhead that slithered into her grave?

In the movie *Bell, Book, and Candle,* Kim Novak portrayed a witch who owned a familiar, a cat named Pywacket. Pywacket is indeed a medieval name for a familiar, as is Greedy-gut, but there is another matter depicted in the film that relates to magic. A little less than thirty minutes into the film, a four piece combo is playing at a night club, supposedly the haunt of modern witches. The combo, one of whom is a bongo player, begins playing closely behind Novak's character at an ever-increasing volume and tempo. The music gets louder and faster until finally his date jumps up, screams, and exits the club. This is described in Gerald B. Gardner's novel *High Magic's Aid.* As I recall the procedure, he asked some ladies who claimed to be witches for a demonstration of magic. The ladies agreed, so long as he would just sit and talk with them. One of the ladies produced a small drum and began slowly to tap it in a quiet rhythm. *[Note: In the movie "Bell, Book, and Candle," the principal instrument was a Bongo drum.]* After a few minutes of talking with all of the women smiling at him and making small talk, he began to feel agitated. The agitation increased. The more agitated he felt and the longer he sat there with those women smiling at him, the more the agitation began to turn to anger, and the madder he became. Finally when he was so angry he could stand it no more, he arose from his chair and called for them to stop. It was then that he realized how the drumming that started out slow and quiet had become faster and faster and louder and louder, raising his blood pressure, all the while the smiling faces of his friends were seeming to mock him, making him angry. The ladies calmed him down and stopped the drumming, and he realized he had just seen an example of magic. Was that really magic? Absolutely not—it was all natural and nothing supernatural was about it. They simply knew how to raise his blood pressure and, likely, his adrenaline by the rhythm of the drum, and they knew a change in his attitude was imminent the longer he sat and was subjected to the drumming. Is there much difference in this than that of Native Americans or natives of African countries who work themselves into a fevered pitch in a war dance to help them kill their enemies? This type of magic is not supernatural but rather has to do with a natural rhythm of the body.

One last note: when I was in college in the sixties and seventies, I did a paper based on the resurgence of spiritualism during and after the Vietnam War. As I accumulated the data, it seemed to me that after every major war in the history of the United States, the popularity of spiritualism resurged, which makes some sense when you realize that significant portions of the population had been killed. At the time I did the research, the increased sales of Ouija boards was one of the indicators. There were others, but alas that information is now lost; however, it could be reassembled if someone wanted to go to the trouble. The desire of relatives wishing to reconnect with their dead loved ones is a great motivator. It is also a real temptation for those charlatans who make a living scamming the unsophisticated, gullible, and heartbroken individuals wanting this reconnection.

Recently, I found an example in an 1865 *Louisville Daily Journal* newspaper article, which seemed to show some evidence of the increase in spiritualism during the American Civil War. General Palmer was in charge of the Kentucky Theater of Operations in 1865 and had his headquarters in Louisville, Kentucky. During the winter of 1865, a guerrilla was captured, one of the last of his kind. He, "One-Armed" Samuel Oscar Berry, was given a court martial and was sentenced to death by hanging; however, another such outlaw, Tom Henry, every bit as guilty, had his death sentence commuted by one of the military courts on a technicality. Palmer said that, in his estimation, both men should have been executed for their depredations. Neither was more nor less guilty than the other. But because the other guerrilla was let off the hook, it did cause Palmer a public relations problem if he executed Berry. By some quirk of fate, a group of ladies from the Louisville Spiritualist Society came to see General Palmer on behalf of Sam Berry. They all agreed that the spirits during a séance had advised them to tell Palmer that he should commute Berry's sentence and allow the prisoner to live. Because of that visit but, more importantly, because of an extended letter writing campaign by supporters of Berry, even including the editor of the "*Louisville Daily Journal*," George Prentice, Palmer commuted Berry's sentence from death to ten years at hard labor. The spiritualists were elated with Palmer's decision to commute Berry's sentence, but Berry died in prison seven years later. He had been shipped off to a federal prison in New York State, where Berry fell victim to an infection in the poor sanitary conditions and died from a fatal disease.

Chapter 19
CONCLUSION

There are two recognized anthropological terms that answer the question of how cultural traits and similarities exist between widely-diverse and geographically-separated societies. The first is diffusion. Diffusion may be defined as the spreading of ideas, religion, technology, and other cultural traits by contact with people from outside their own culture. Traders, travelers, hunting parties, and visiting strangers see something one culture is doing that seems like a good idea, and they carry that idea or trait to their own or other societies, where it is duplicated or modified to better serve that new group. People who interact with that new group on a periodic basis see and accept the concept and further spread it by additional human contact. In this way over an area as large as a continent, ideas can be disseminated across great distances. Of course, this may take thousands of years to happen, and it is diffused differently in Europe than the Americas. Diffusion in the Eastern Hemisphere is east to west, and in the Americas, it is from north to south. This is decided by the east to west mountain ranges in the Eastern Hemisphere, which allow relatively unimpeded travel and similar climactic environments along latitudinal lines. In the Americas, the mountain ranges are north to south, meaning diffusion is along longitudinal lines, impeding coast-to-coast transmission of these traits. Since similar plants grow along latitudinal lines where the climate is more uniform, Asian and European culture evolved more rapidly than in the Americas because the coast-to-coast diffusion was unimpeded in one hemisphere and impeded in the other. The bow and arrow was invented in the Eastern Hemisphere 30,000 years B.P., but in the Western Hemisphere it was invented 3,000 years B.P. This isolation may well be part of the reason witch beliefs and superstitions continue to exist in the Appalachians. The diffusion theory does not account for the spread of ideas and innovations between continents at a time when intercontinental travel was unlikely. At that point, another term may explain similarities between certain African cultures and North or South American cultures or any of a host of other comparisons of traits in distant societies that can be similarly made. That anthropological term is multi-linear evolution.

Multi-linear evolution accounts for environmental causes and effects and results in the development of similar industries, tools, dress, and other cultural traits between people separated by vast distances and natural barriers, such as oceans and mountain ranges, that are presumably too far removed and difficult to cross for these similarities to be the result of diffusion. The similar innovations are driven solely by need, natural resources, and environmental conditions, such as climate, temperature, latitude, and population. The pyramids of Egypt and those of the Mayan and Aztecs come to mind when we consider the proposition of multi-linear evolution as examples of similar ideas originating with peoples widely separated and, presumably, not in contact with each other who conceive similar structures, or traits.

Other comparisons can be made of stone tool morphology and variability, ceramics (pottery), dress, and more. This concept of like ideas developing in far-flung cultures with similar environmental factors, such as climate, vegetation, mineral, and animal resources, explain much better why similar industries designed to exploit that environment took place. It makes more sense, I think, than using pseudo-scientific theories, such as the ideas being spread across the Earth by aliens from outer space, no matter how much fun those theories might be. It is interesting to me (and germane to the subject of this book) that there is one universal belief in all known societies irrespective of diffusion or multi-linear evolution and that belief is in witchcraft or sorcery. Sometimes, the supernatural beliefs in sorcery, witchcraft, and Devil are comingled with supernatural religious concepts, such as the dichotomy of good and evil in the religions or in the acknowledgment of an anthropomorphic Devil by most Christian denominations, including the rites of exorcism still intact and sometimes practiced by the Roman Catholic Church. In anthropology, the concept of religion is not separate and apart from a belief in witchcraft and sorcery. Societies with less sophisticated socioeconomic systems may accept the proposition that they are co-equal. That seems to be the case in the minds of some Native American, American, and African traditions. Anthropologically-speaking, it is customary to define religion in terms of man's relationship to the supernatural. Religion also has to do with those things that are outside and beyond the areas of man's practical control *and witchcraft and sorcery are regarded as evil and profane* [emphasis mine]. Others see religion as an expression, in one form or another, of a sense of dependence on a supernatural power (God) outside of ourselves that can be thought of as a spiritual moral force. Any attempt to define religion as supernatural, which it anthropologically is, raises the question of what is the difference between religion as supernatural and witchcraft and sorcery as supernatural. I believe witchcraft and sorcery, which are almost universally regarded as evil, *wicked or twisted,* [emphasis mine] are a part of religion only in the sense that they are ways of accounting for the evil forces and their power in the world. But even if we limit magic to its beneficent and socially-approved aspects, the problem *of separation between them,* [emphasis mine] remains.[116]

The fact that witchcraft and magic can co-exist with religion, even in a negative way and may even be merged at times could explain how Blymire, Leah, Leah's mother, and many other faith healers who effect beneficial relief or cures for their patients with only their hands and a prayer can be perceived as working magic. When the results do not work to the benefit of the society, the healer fails and the patient worsens or dies. It is not much of a stretch to see how the perception of the practitioner might change in a negative fashion to the detriment of the healer. I think this may have happened to Leah Smock.

Are there really good and bad witches? Glenda, the good witch in *The Wizard of Oz,* was certainly different than her sister, who was crushed by the house. She was beautiful and benevolent, and her sister was cruel and mean, but *was* she really different? It seems if you do good things then you are a good witch; conversely, if you do bad things, you are a bad one. I was told those who practiced the Old Religion believe whatever they did in this life would be returned threefold in their next life. Witches are supposed to believe in reincarnation. This leaves us with the proposition that if one did a lot of good and a little bad, the bad things they did would be of little consequence later. I suppose, acting under this premise, if you did a lot of really good things, you could curse and kill one or two people without much of a consequence. I liken this to being able to write one's own writ of indulgence. It flies in the face of almost all universally-recognized religious beliefs.

The Christian View

We have seen how the Christian Church has constructed some of its sacraments, holy days, ceremonies, and belief system based, at least in part, on pagan practices in play before Jesus was born. A fact that must be clear is that Christianity developed into a religion amidst a lurid pagan environment, which could not fail to have its influence upon the new faith.[117] I do believe that someplace along the line of its development, the simple teachings of Christianity have been obscured. They are still there but hidden within the trappings that seemed necessary to convert the pagans to Christianity and, for some, became the focal point of the Christian religion. But are these simple basic truths that Jesus preached and lived by example as viable today as they were on April 6, A.D. 30. What are those truths? The Jesus of history, as distinct from the Jesus of theology, remains "the way, the truth, and the life." Arthur Weigall wrote, "I am convinced that concentration upon the historic figure of our Jesus and upon His teaching can alone inspire in this 21st century".[118] The original Christians believed Jesus to be the incarnate Son of God, largely because they were convinced that, after being sacrificially crucified, His dead body had come to life again. He appeared to them in the flesh after they had seen Him die on the cross.[119] The sacrificial nature of the crucifixion, the sacraments' value of the Passion, became astonishingly plain, but this interpretation would not have been so immediately apparent had there not been these prehistoric beliefs to prepare the mind for the revelation. Jesus not only fulfilled the Judaic scriptures, but He also fulfilled those of the pagan world. In Him, a dozen shadowy gods were condensed into a proximate reality, and in His crucifixion, the old stories of their ghastly atoning sufferings and sacrificial deaths were made actual and were given direct meaning.[120] In A. D. 64, Peter, the only living man who knew Jesus, or Peter's secretary personally describes him as One Who—

> "suffered...leaving us an example...who did no sin, neither was guile found in his mouth: who, when he reviled, reviled not again; when he suffered, he threatened not, but

committed himself to Him that judgeth righteously: who,
His own self bore our sins in His own body on the tree...by
whose stripes we are healed."[121]

He was gone to heaven but would soon return. In order to follow
the example of Jesus, Peter urges his readers to love one another, to
be compassionate, piteous, courteous; to not render evil for evil but
meet insults with blessings; to be charitable, hospitable, humble; to do
good, to eschew evil, and to seek peace; to abstain from lusts of the
flesh, to avoid malice, envy, and evil speaking; to submit to authority, to fear God and honor the King; to accept blows and reproaches
for righteousness' sake; and, above all, to receive the faith like little
children, trusting in God's mercy.[122] Weigall states, "this is the earliest
revelation of the surprisingly beautiful character of Jesus that we possess...written without doubt by one that knew him." These are the true
teachings of Jesus.

I planned to write this book to explain what happened to Leah by
framing her story in the context of the time and the social, economic,
and religious environment in which she lived. I found in that explanation that any sorcery she practiced or power she held was probably
natural and did not exist at all. This does not explain away the things
that happened after her death. There are simply too many odd events
and sightings and too much evidence that her spirit continues to linger
and haunt the region. How can one explain that? In 2015, a Meade
County woman named Kay Hamilton, who worked in the Battletown
Elementary School as the school secretary, wrote a book entitled *A
Ghost In Our School*. In it, she documented appearances of appari-
tions of a woman dressed in the same style and manner described in
the accounts of those people who first saw Leah after she was buried. There were numerous visual and audible examples of the spirit in
that school. The Battletown School, now closed, sits very close to or,
perhaps, on part of the John and Elizabeth Smock property. Linger-
ing perfume from the ghost, flitting shadows, and the uneasy sense
of someone being present when nothing was there indicates the presence of a female spirit. The apparition of a young lady in 1800s garb,
who is sensed by a dog's keen sense of smell or knowing, makes the
supernatural connection to Leah logical. When you think of Leah being attracted to school and no doubt wandering that area of the hills

and hollows of old Meade, it gives rise to the possibility. Kay Hamilton asks the question, "Could the apparition really be Leah Smock? Could she have been drawn to the school by the voices and laughter of the children? Do all of our experiences stem from one ghost or were there multiple ghosts?"[123] Whether or not Leah was a witch and whether her spirit lingered in the school and the area of Battletown today cannot be definitely answered; even so, that society and environment witnessed the burning of Leah Smock. To understand this phenomenon, I feel it's necessary to understand how witchcraft in America was influenced by Western European, Native American, and African pagan practices. Developing in the geographic isolation of the Appalachians, it held tenuous connections to Christianity and the ancient superstitions of these influential cultures. Leah and Margaret Smock, Mary Reynolds, John Blymire, and others were considered by their community to be Christian, church-going people endowed by God with special gifts or talents. The pagan traditions allowed into the early Christian Church made the church stronger, not for Christianity to become pagan-like but rather to convert the pagans to Christianity. This led to creation of dates for Christ's unknown birth, circumcision, baptism, ascension, and to bring into the faith the female element of Mary, the mother of God, all of which may be based, in part, upon pre-Christian pagan traditions.

The Christian impulse is one of faith, love, hope, and charity, and all the things that the historic Jesus taught and exemplified while He walked upon the earth. While there is no doubt that many pagan traditions and holy days have become embedded in Christian theology, over the years these traditions have been so ingrained into the Christian faith to the point that on December 25 our thoughts turn to the birth of Christ and not Mithra. The gifts of the Magi to Jesus are celebrated with Christmas gift-giving, and the Christmas tree isn't thought of in terms of the rebirth because it is now incorporated into the Christian Christmas tradition. Isn't that the way it's supposed to be? It must be because that's the way it has become.

Afterword

This book would not have been possible without the input and assistance of Shirley Brown of Wolf Creek, Kentucky. Shirley is not only the great-great niece of Leah Smock but has also shared her insight and family lore pertaining to Leah. She has shared stories and personal papers and her skill as a photographer in this tribute to Leah. Writing the book has proven to be a great adventure, and I hope it provides clarity and explains somewhat why the events of August 1840 took place. It isn't meant to prove or disprove whether or not Leah and her mother Margaret were witches but rather to offer explanations as to why the killing of Leah took place. Leah was a beautiful, intelligent, independent, and perhaps headstrong girl whose ability to firmly deal with her neighbors made them, in the end, fear her. Within a radius of eighty to two hundred miles, documented witchcraft incidents predate the Leah Smock lynching by twenty-seven years. From then until 1929, when an actual trial for murder took place in the United States with one alleged witch killing another, other instances of witchcraft occurred.

There are many natural occurrences described in this book that appear to be magical but aren't. They are, for the most part, predictable events based on knowledge of nature and the observance of the physical world. Today, we have specialists to forecast the weather. We needn't heed the katydid's call. With future scientific innovations, there may be greater, technological advancement, through the use of which we may explain away the supernatural.

Considering technology and the supernatural, there is something else that I think needs to be considered. In 1965 and earlier, there were few paranormal ghost hunters who weren't, for the most part, spiritualistic mediums. There were few photographs of spirits that could stand up to scrutiny, and to my knowledge, there were no recording devices that could easily be applied to ghost hunting as there are today. There must be a half dozen or more paranormal shows on television now. Special features on the History Channel, Discovery Channel, or other stations are devoted to explaining spectral images of mists and orbs and playing recordings of ghosts or spirits speaking. Technology has advanced to a point that, with the use of digital equipment, spectral entities are able to be detected and recorded. To be sure while preparing this book, we have experienced some familiarity with ghostly phenomena.

In October of 2011, Shirley Brown was giving a presentation at the Meade County Public Library about her famous great-great-great-aunt, Leah Smock. Her presentation occurred on the same evening as our MCHAPS meeting, where we had a lady, Diana Burnett, who was the historian at Camp Carlson, Fort Knox, Kentucky, to address the society. This lady had experienced a ghostly paranormal event while doing an archaeological investigation at the old elementary school in Grayhampton, a ghost town that became Camp Carlson when Fort Knox expanded its boundary and bought the town in the 1940s. She was excavating around the old school building's foundation, carefully digging with a trowel and sifting the soil for artifacts. She had her back to the road, across which lay a field that was kept mowed so that children of the campers would have a safe place to play away from traffic. She was about halfway down the foundation when she heard a group of boys and girls behind her begin a baseball game. They chose up sides, and she could hear the whack of the bat against the balls. She could hear the pounding of feet as they ran around the bases. There were sounds of cheers from the people watching the game, and there were sounds of derision from one side when the other team did something good. She was enjoying the sounds of the kids while she was doing the excavation. When she reached the back corner of the building and had to turn ninety degrees to the left to follow the rear wall, she decided to stand up and watch the game. She could hear the game being played as she arose, but when she turned toward the field, the sounds stopped, and there were no children on the field. It was quiet, and she was alone. Diana said she was badly frightened and ran several blocks to the building that housed the office. When she got there, still shaking from the fright, her boss said, "I'm glad you're here. I have something to show you." Diana replied, "No, I've got to tell you what just happened." Her boss insisted he show her what he found before she told him her story. He told her that he knew she was working on the excavation of the school building, and he produced a photograph of the school he had just found, dating from the 1920s or 1930s. A ball game was being played in the field across the road from the school. Coincidence, paranormal, or extrasensory—you decide.

When our meeting ended, Shirley's presentation was ending at the same time. As we all exited from the meeting rooms across the common area, Shirley said that she wanted to introduce me to some people. I was delighted to meet a new reporter from the *Messenger*, our weekly newspaper, and three women from a group of ghost hunters. These ghost hunters used the latest technology. Since at that time, I organized most of our meetings, I immediately asked them to give a presentation to MCHAPS at our October meeting, and they did.

During the month of August 2012, I took these ladies to cemeteries and other places where Civil War raids, murders, and ambuscades took place. They made recordings and measured the electrical impulses at several cemeteries and various sites where people violently died. The voice recordings were played for the membership at our meeting, and several photographs were shown that contained mists and orbs. It was a great meeting, and everyone was impressed by what these ladies had found.

Later at another meeting in October of 2014, Danielle and Steve hosted a ghost hunt at a store where some paranormal activities had recently occurred. The results were fascinating and a little bit scary. It is with the use of this new equipment, coupled with competent technicians, that progress seems to be made toward a rational explanation of these paranormal events. I mention this because, as technology advances and can be applied to the study of predicting the future or in discerning subtle changes in the environment, aura, or atmosphere around those that can heal or cure the thrush or stop bleeding, perhaps we can better understand at least the physical nature of these things. On reflection, though, wouldn't that remove the romance and mystery these deeds inspire in our lives, which reinforces our faith in a mystical, positive moral power greater than ourselves who works through these people chosen to heal the sick? And, if that happened, would we not be the poorer for having the mystery removed?

AN EXPEDITION
TO LEAH'S GRAVE

O n January 7, 2016, five of us met at Kays and Joe Mack Hamilton's house to visit Leah's grave. Shirley Brown, Kay, Joe, and I made the trip to the cemetery. It was every bit the arduous journey described on the telephone to me years earlier. We drove in a truck to a pull-off, where Joe had an off-road, 4-wheel-drive ATV to begin the trip. He made trips back and forth of at least a half mile, ferrying each of us to a place where we could begin the hike to the cemetery. We parked the ATV at a former saw mill operation that terminated on the rough dirt road at a wet weather creek. Assembled there, we crossed the rocky creek bed and climbed the opposite bank to a creek-bottom field. Across the field, we followed a logging road for a hundred yards or so and came to another abandoned saw mill operation at the intersection with yet another dirt road. We were in a hardwood forest for most of the hike until we emerged into a field that abutted the same creek some distance further. There were pockets of water standing in small pools along the creek bed from a heavy rain a week earlier, and as we walked into the field dotted with deer beds, we saw many of their tracks. We continuously encountered sawgrass and briars, typical of wild Kentucky land, along the way. The day was clear, and the weather balmy with light breezes. From this point, Kay suggested we wait while she scouted ahead for the best route to the cemetery. Joe, Shirley, and I found a suitable log on which to sit while we waited. After some twenty minutes or so, we heard a far-off voice call, but we could not make out if it was Kay or what words it was saying. We started toward the sound of the voice through the woods along what we thought was a continuation of the log road we had just hiked. The geology changed. Now, we could see outcroppings of limestone rocks and more Eastern red cedar and loblolly pine trees, indicators of underlying limestone. We were walking up hill and saw Kay with a big smile on her face coming to meet us. She had found the cemetery. We walked another hundred yards or so to a small clearing and around its perimeter to where a dirt road entered the woods to the north. As we walked along the road upwardly to a small knoll, the Betsy Daily tombstones loomed into view on our left. The cemetery is in the midst of a forested area with a ground cover I know as mourning ivy. It is often found in old Kentucky cemeteries. There are reputed to be some eighty graves in the cemetery, and there is all measure of stones, from simple field stones to ones elaborately carved and engraved.

The cemetery was abandoned in the 1920s, and except for occasional decoration days or hunters passing through the area, it is a lonesome place. The graves are arranged east to west in a somewhat confusing way. Most Protestant and Catholic cemeteries bury with the head of the deceased facing east to the rising sun. The inscriptions are usually on the east side of the stone. In this cemetery, there are stones with the inscriptions on the east, and some with the inscriptions on the west. Customarily and in most cemeteries I have visited, the stones are generally facing in one direction or another, thus making this either/or arrangement unusual.

While Kay was searching amongst the stones for Leah's grave, Shirley, Joe, and I were carefully walking through the stones while vines, depressions, and unseen field stones seemed to try to trip us. Kay called out when she had found the grave. Carefully making our way to her, we all stood at Leah's grave in quiet contemplation, and for a brief moment, no one said a word. Shirley, like me, had never been to Leah's grave, but unlike me, she was a distant niece of Leah's. We noted some things right off. The inscription on Leah's grave was on the west side of her stone. We assumed that she was buried facing the setting sun, unusual for a Christian cemetery; however, there was no settlement depression to the west nor was there any stones we should have encountered on top of her grave. I noticed a slight rise on the east side of her tombstone, and with my walking stick, I found they were remnants of field stones, almost invisible due to the mourning ivy and leaf litter that covers the cemetery. These stones were placed by the men who dug down into her grave and filled it with them, stacked three feet above the ground. This was done after Leah Smock's ghost was seen standing at her grave and in an effort to keep her from arising from it. Now the stones are perhaps six or eight inches above the ground. Settlement has no doubt caused some stones to sink into the grave and souvenir hunters, possibly to their detriment, have removed others. We discussed the placement of Leah's tombstone and inscription, trying to determine what it meant. In my mind, there is a simple and practical reason for her stone to have the engraving facing west while her body was buried by her family presumably facing east. Reflecting on this matter, I believe we have to go back to the legend and consider what may have caused this odd placement. According to the legend, it took Leah's boyfriend some time to find just the right stone and then to shape and engrave it. This may have taken a month or more to do. I say this because most of the common Meade County limestone outcroppings are boulders or irregularly-shaped nodules. Limestone is a sedimentary rock lain down as an ocean floor millions of years ago, but finding it layered in the approximate three inch thickness is not common. Shale and slate are often found in that confirmation but not the naturally-occurring limestone in our area. If her boyfriend took a chunk of limestone and chiseled it to that uniform thickness, it would have taken a long time. To search for an uncommon piece of that even thickness, allowing time for dressing the edges and engraving, would also have taken quite some time. The legend states that a hunter saw her apparition standing over her grave a week after her burial. He likely told about what he saw as soon as he could, and fear spurred the others to quick action, probably her killers who had the most to fear from her. They loaded two wagons with rocks, likely taking a week or two, drove them to her grave, dug into it, and filled it with stones to a height three feet above the ground. Leah's tombstone is about thirty inches high, but the engraving is lower. It is about twenty-four inches in width, but typically, a grave is four feet wide. Taking all things into account, her boyfriend most likely arrived to set her stone after her grave was filled with rocks. Had he placed the engraving toward the east, it would not have been visible, hidden by a four foot wide pile of rocks three feet high. Faced with this situation, he probably placed the stone with the engraving facing west where people could identify her. There could, of course, be other reasons.

Shirley read a heartfelt poem to Leah, and we took photographs commemorating our visit. My wife Fran, who could not make the walk, waited at Kay's house but brought flowers for Shirley to decorate the grave of this woman brutally murdered in 1840. Carefully and reverently, we all watched as Shirley laid the flowers on her grave. While I can't speak for everyone, I know I said a little prayer and hoped Leah was listening. I think we all did.

Genealogy of Leah Smock from 1818 until Present

Father: John Smock

Born: 16 May 1797   in: New Jersey
Married: About 1815   in: Unknown
Died: 11 February 1876   in: Unknown
Burial: in: Cunningham Cemetery, Wolf Creek, Ky.

Mother: Margaret Ann (Maiden name unknown)

Born: 1796   in: Pennsylvania
Died: 3 June 1889   in: Unknown
Burial: in: Possibly Meade County

Children:

Name: Elizabeth Ann Smock
     Born: 26 July 1835   in: Indiana
     Died: 28 October 1882   in: Meade County, Kentucky
     Burial: in: Cunningham Cemetery, Wolf Creek, Ky.
     Married: 25 October 1855   in: by Fr. Patrick McNichols, (Catholic Priest)
     Spouse: Israel Allen
     Married: 16 January 1868   in: Meade County, Ky., by Rev. John S. Willett
     Spouse: Blandford Ballard
Name: Joseph T. Smock
     Born: About 1825   in: Virginia
     Married: in: Unknown
     Died: in: Unknown

Name: Leah Smock
Born: January 1818   in: Unknown
Died: 21 August 1840   in: Meade County, Ky.
Burial: in: Betsy Daily Cemetery,
                                Battletown, Ky.

Husband of Elizabeth Ann Smock: Israel Allen

Born: About 1821   in: Unknown
Married: 25 October 1855 in: by Fr. Patrick McNichols
                                (Catholic Priest)

Died: Between 1862 and 1867 in: Unknown
Father: Unknown Allen
Mother: Marcy Unknown
Other Spouses: Sarah A. Devore

Children:

Name: Cassandra Allen
Born: 9 June 1856   in: Unknown
Married: in: Unknown
Died: in: Unknown
Burial: in: Unknown
Spouse: in: Unknown
Name: Eliza Jane Allen
Born: 1856   in: Unknown
Married: in: Unknown
Died: in: Unknown
Burial: in: Unknown
Spouse: in: Unknown
Name: Ida G. Allen
Born: 1862   in: Unknown
Married: in: Unknown
Died: in: Unknown
Burial: in: Unknown
Spouse: in: Unknown

Husband: Blanford Ballard

Born: About 1835   in: Indiana
Married: 16 January 1868 in: Meade County, Ky. by
                                Rev. John S. Willett

Died: 17 April 1897   in: Unknown
Father: Blanford Ballard
Mother: Lucinda Etherton
Other Spouses:

Wife: Elizabeth Ann Smock
Born: 26 July 1835   in: Indiana
Died: 28 October 1882   in: Meade County, Ky.
Burial: in: Cunningham Cemetery,
                                           Wolf Creek, Ky.

Father: John Smock
Mother: Margaret Ann Unknown
Other Spouses: Israel Allen

Children:
Name: Arigusta Ballard
Born: 22 February 1871   in: Unknown
Died: 8 February 1901   in: Unknown
Burial: in: Bald Knob Cemetery,
                                           Battletown, Ky.

Married: 20 December 1888   in: Meade County, Ky., by
                                           B.F. Singleton

Spouse: John Shoemaker Singleton
Name: John W. Ballard
Born: About 1869   in: Unknown
Married: in: Unknown
Died: in: Unknown
Burial: in: Unknown
Spouse:
Name: Josephine T. Ballard
Born: 22 February 1874   in: Unknown
Died: 1900   in: Unknown
Burial: in: Unknown
Married: 9 February 1893   in: Unknown
Spouse: James Edward Stewart
Name: Eugene Ballard
Born: 19 July 1877   in: Unknown
Died: 19 June 1937   in: Unknown

Burial:	in: Riley, Bullock, Finch,
	Cem., Wolf Creek, Ky.
Married:	in: Unknown
Spouse: Nora Dell Troutman	
Name: Clarence Ballard	
Born 25 May 1880	in: Indiana
Married:	in: Unknown
Died: 7 December 1892	in: Unknown
Burial:	in: Unknown
Spouse:	

Husband: John Shoemaker Singleton

Born: 12 June 1865	in: Meade County, Ky.
Married: 20 December 1888	in: Meade County. Ky., by B.F.
	Singleton
Died: 12 April 1943	in: Meade County, Ky.
Burial:	in: Parr-Frans Cemetery,
	Meade County, Ky.

Father: William Henry Harrison Singleton
Mother: Elizabeth Baysinger
Other Spouses:

Wife: Arigusta Ballard

Born: 22 February 1871	in: Unknown
Died: 8 February 1901	in: Unknown
Burial:	in: Bald Knob Cemetery,
	Battletown, Ky.

Father: Blanford Ballard
Mother: Elizabeth Ann Smock
Other Spouses:

Children:

Name: Bertha Elizabeth Singleton

Born: 22 October 1890	in: Unknown
Died: 1 September 1987	in: Unknown
Burial:	in: Parr-Frans Cemetery,
	Wolf Creek, Ky.
Married: 22 October 1911	in: Meade County, Ky., By
	James B. Hayes
Spouse: Nathan Troutman	

Name: Della Ethel Singleton
    Born 26 February 1892   in: Wolf Creek, Ky.
    Died: 22 March 1989   in: Hardin Memorial Hosp.
                                Elizabethtown, Ky.

    Burial: 24 March 1989   in: Parr-Frans Cemetery,
                                Wolf Creek, Ky.

    Married: 8 November 1908   in: Wolf Creek, Ky., By Rev.
                                John S. Willett

    Spouse: John William Troutman
Name: Eugene Marshall Singleton
    Born: 10 October 1893   in: Unknown
    Died: 3 February 1982   in: Hancock County, Ky.
    Burial: in: Unknown
    Married: 25 October 1914   in: Unknown
    Spouse: Dorothy Curl
Name: Lawrence Albert Singleton
    Born: 24 August 1895   in: Unknown
    Died: 8 July 1981   in: Unknown
    Burial: in: Parr-Frans Cemetery,
                                Battletown, Ky.

    Married: 11 May 1919   in: Unknown
    Spouse: Fayme Nell Pleasant in: Unknown
    Married: After 1952   in: Unknown
    Spouse: Beulah Frances Turner
Name: Cora Ellen Singleton
    Born: About 1897   in: Unknown
    Married: in: Unknown
    Died: 13 March 1900   in: Unknown
    Burial: in: Bald Knob Cemetery,
                                Battletown, Ky.

    Spouse:
Name: Otis Avery Singleton
    Born: 11 August 1898   in: Unknown
    Died: 12 November 1961   in: Lewisport, Ky.
    Burial: in: Unknown
    Married: 21 September 1922 in: Unknown
    Spouse: Ruth E. Curl

Name: Alvin Beckham Singleton
  Born: 11 October 1900   in: Unknown
  Died: 7 November 1937   in: Unknown
  Burial: in: Unknown
  Married: 30 September 1922   in: Unknown
  Spouse: Zelpha Pearl Ammons

Husband: *John William Troutman*
  Born: 4 February 1872   in: Meade County, Ky.
  Married: 8 November 1908   in: Wolf Creek, By Rev. John
                                   S. Willett
  Died: 15 January 1961   in: Breckenridge Mem.
                                   Hospital, Hardinsburg,
                                   Ky.
  Burial: 17 January 1961   in: Parr Cemetery, Wolf
                                   Creek, Ky.
  Father: Benjamin Franklin Troutman
  Mother: Sarah Catherine Curl

Wife: *Della Ethel Singleton*
  Born: 26 February 1892   in: Wolf Creek, Meade
                                   County, Ky.
  Died: 22 March 1989   in: Hardin Memorial Hospital,
                                   Elizabethtown, Ky.
  Burial: 24 March 1989   in: Parr Cemetery
  Father: John Shoemaker Singleton
  Mother: Arigusta Ballard
  Other Spouses:

Children: *Annabelle Troutman*
  Born: 15 April 1914   in: Meade County, Ky.
  Died: 31 July 2004   in: Wolf Creek, Meade
                                   County, Ky.
  Burial: 4 August 2004   in: Parr-Frans Cemetery,
                                   Battletown, Ky.
  Married: 28 June   in: Louisville, Ky., by Rev.
                                   D.L. Burnett's home
  Spouse: Sherley Eugene Vandiver
Name: Nellie Mabel Troutman
  Born: 7 August 1911   in: Unknown

Died: 20 January 1994   in: Hardin Memorial Hospital,
Elizabethtown, Ky.

Burial: in: Parr-Frans Cemetery,
Battletown, Ky.

Married: 6 July 1929   in: Louisville, Ky. Rev. D. L.
Burnett's home

Spouse: Raymond Wesley Chism
Name: Joseph Lawrence Troutman
Born: 21 June 1921   in: Concordia, Meade
County, Ky.

Died: in:
Burial: in:
Married: 9 August 1945   in: Madison, Wisconsin
Spouse: Myriam Lois Berger
Married: 17 June 1995   in: Hilltop Lakes, Texas
Spouse: Charlotte Meadows
Husband: Sherley Eugene Vandiver
Born: 24 February 1913   in: Meade County, Ky.
Married: 28 June 1941   in: Louisville, Ky., Rev. D. L.
Barnett's home

Died: 27 November 1969   in: St. Josephs Infirmary,
Louisville, Ky.

Burial: in: Parr-Frans Cemetery,
Meade County, Ky.

Father: Richard Martin Vandiver
Mother: Cora Ethel Chism
Other Spouses:
Wife: Annabelle Troutman
Born: 15 April 1914   in: Meade County, Ky.
Died: 31 July 2004   in: Wolf Creek, Meade
County, Ky.

Burial: 4 August 2004   in: Parr-Frans Cemetery,
Meade County, Ky.

Father: John William Troutman
Mother: Della Ethel Singleton
Other Spouses:
Children:
Name: * *Shirley Ann Vandiver*

Born: 5 October 1945, 2:30 p.m.   in: Meade County, Ky.
Died:
Burial:
Married: 19 December 1965   in: Wolf Creek Baptist Ch.,
                                     Wolf Creek, Ky.

Spouse: Paul Lewis Ellis
Married: 30 June 1984   in: Meade Co. Rescue
                                 Grnds., Payneville, Ky.

Spouse: James Alan Kline
Married: 1 July 1994   in: Wolf Creek Baptist Ch.,
                                Wolf Creek, Ky.

Spouse: Zane Baxter Brown
Name: John Richard Vandiver
Born: 17 October 1942   in: Roberta Community,
                                 Meade County, Ky.

Died: 16 December 2015
Burial:
Married: 30 December 1964
Spouse: Margaret Pauline Craven
Married: 6 April 1993   in: Tarrant, Texas
Spouse: Bernice Craven

*Shirley Vandiver Brown is the great-great-niece of Leah Smock and was born in Wolf Creek, Kentucky, in October 1945. She first attended Cedar Flat School, where her mother was a teacher. She graduated from Meade County High School in 1963, and she enjoys photography, reading, gardening, crafts, genealogy, and history. Her sunrise and storm pictures have been shown numerous times on television and are on display at the University of Kentucky's Meade County Extension office. Shirley is a certified firefighter with the Wolf Creek Fire Department. She has taught Sunday school for fifty years, is a member of the Meade County Historical and Archaeological Preservation Society, and is a Red Hatter. She mostly enjoys spending time with her two children, six grandchildren, and five great-grandchildren. She shared family papers, stories, photographs, and newspaper articles and clippings referenced this book.

References

Adams, Richard C. *Legends of the Delaware Indians and Picture Writing,* Syracuse, New York: Syracuse University Press 2000.

Schwatka, Frederick. *Among The Apaches.* Palmer Lake, Colorado: The Filter Press, 1974.

Beattie, John, *Bunyoro. An African Kingdom.* Stanford University, San Jose, California, United States, Holt, Rinehart, Winston, 1960.

Binford, Sallie R., and Binford, Lewis R. *New Perspectives in Archaeology,* Aldine Publishing Co., Chicago, 1968.

Bordaz, Jacques. *Tools Of The Old And New Stone Age.* Garden City, New York: The American Museum of Natural History, The Natural History Press, 1970.

Bordes, Francois. *A Tale Of Two Caves.* New York: Harper Row Publishers, 1972.

Browne, Corinne. *Understanding Other Cultures.* Englewood Cliffs, New Jersey: Prentice Hall, 1963.

Buckland, Raymond. *Ancient and Modern Witchcraft.* New York: H. C. Publishers Inc., 1970.

---. *Witchcraft the Religion.* New York: The Buckland Museum of Witchcraft & Magick, Inc., New York, 1966.

Cottrell, Arthur, and Rachael Storm. *Illustrated Encyclopedia of World Mythology.* New York: Metro Books, 2013.

Constabe, George. *The Neanderthals.* New York: Time Life Books, 1973.

Dorland, W. A. Newman. *American Pocket Medical Dictionary,* 16th ed. Philadelphia: W. B. Saunders Company, 1940.

Downs, James F. Downs. *Two Worlds Of The Washo.* New York: Holt, Rinehart And Winston, 1966.

Farrar, Stewart. *What Witches Do*. New York: Coward, McCann & Geohegan, Inc., 1971.

Fetrow, Charles W. and Avila, Juan R. *The Complete Guide To Herbal Remedies*. New York: Pocket Books, 2000.

Gaddis, Vincent H. *American Indian Myths and Legends*. New York: Signet, 1977.

Gardner, Gerald B. *The Meaning of Witchcraft*, Whitstable, England: Latimer Trend & Co. Ltd., 1959.

Grammery, Ann. *The Witches Workbook*. New York: Pocket Books, 1973.

Jahoda, Gustav. *The Psychology Of Superstition*. Harmondsworth, England: Penguin Books, 1970.

Johns, June. *King of the Witches*. New York: Coward-McCann, Inc., 1969.

Glass, Justine. *Witchcraft, Sixth Sense*, Hollywood, CA: Wilshire Book Company, 1970.

Geronimo, as told to Barrett, S. M.. *Geronimo His Own Story*. Harmondsworth, England: Meridan, 1996.

Graves, Robert. *The White Goddess*. 6th ed. New York: Farrar, N. V., Straus and Giroux, 1948.

Hamilton, Kay. *A Ghost In Our School*. Brandenburg, Kentucky: Bearhead Publishing, 2015.

Klein, Richard G. *Ice-Age Hunters of the Ukraine*. Chicago: University of Chicago Press, 1973.

Kroeber, Theodora. *Ishi Last of His Tribe*. New York: Bantam Books, 1973.

Lady Sheba, *The Book of Shadows*. St. Paul, MN: Lewellyn Publications, 1971.

Lewis, Arthur H. *Hex* New York: Trident Press, 1969.

Lewis, Thomas M. N. and Madeline Kneberg. *Tribes That Slumber*. Knoxville, TN: The University of Tennessee Press, 1958.

Mair, Lucy. *Witchcraft*. New York: McGraw Hill, 1969.

Malachi, Martin. *Decline and Fall of the Roman Church*. New York: Bantam, 1983.

Merriam-Webster's Collegiate Dictionary Tenth Edition. Springfield, Massachusetts: Merriam-Webster, Inc., 2002.

Neill, Wilfred T. *Florida's Seminole Indians*. St. Petersburg, FL: Great Outdoors, 1956.

Oakley, Kenneth P. *Man The Tool Maker*. Chicago: Phoenix Books, The University Of Chicago Press, 1962.

Peterson, Roger Troy. *Peterson First Guide to Wildflowers of North America*. New York: Houghton Mifflin Company, 1987.

Rose, Ronald. *Living Magic*. New York: Rand McNally & Company, 1956.

Scott, Sir Walter. *Letters On Demonology & Witchcraft*. New York: Ace Publishing Corporation, 1970.

Sepherial. *The Book of Charms and Talismans*. New York: ARC Books, Inc., 1969.

Simmonite, William Joseph and Culpepper, Nicholas. The *Simmonite-Culpepper Herbal Remedies*. New York: W. Foulsham & Co. Ltd. New York, 1957

Smith, Susy. *Prominent American Ghosts*. New York: The World Publishing Company, 1967.

Spence, Lewis. *Magic Arts in Celtic Britain*. London: Samuel Weiser Inc., Aquarian Press, 1970.

Sprenger, Jacobus, and Kramer, Heinrich. *Malleus Maleficarum*. London: The Folio Society, 1968.

Weigall, Arthur. *The Paganism in our Christianity*. New York: G. P. Putnam's Sons, 1928.

Wendt, Herbert. *In Search of Adam*. Boston: Houghton Mifflin Company, 1956.

Wiggenton, Eliot. *The Foxfire Book*. New York: Anchor Books, DOUBLEDAY, 1986.

---. *Foxfire 9*. New York: Anchor Books, DOUBLEDAY, 1986.

Wong, James. *Grow Your Own Drugs*. Pleasantville, NY: The Reader's Digest Association, Inc., 2009.

Periodicals

Gerald W. Fischer. "The Bryant Family and the Last Indian War in Minnesota." *Kentucky Explorer* 28, no. 4. (September 2013).

"Rebuilding Your Health With Herbs and Natural Foods." *Healthful Living Digest*. 32, no. 1. (1972).

New Dimensions. May. Gloucestershire, England: Helios Book Service, 1964.

The Witches' Almanac, from Aires 1971 to Pisces 1972, New York: Grosset & Dunlap, 1972.

Articles and Papers

"Religion." *Life Magazine*. October 1964.

Thain. "Witchcraft 1968." *Search Magazine*. Wisconsin. January 1968.

Fischer, Gerald W. "Witchcraft: The Evolution of A Neolithic Fertility Cult to 1400 A. D." University of Louisville (Spring 1972).

The Shirley Brown Family Papers and genealogy, Shirley Brown and JoAnne Willett

The Gerald Fischer Family Papers. Mortgage of to A. C. Bryant. March 8, 1946. Bowling Green, Kentucky.

Poetry

Furnival, Beverly. "The Ballad of Leah Smock," 2012.

Haugen, Marty. "The Canticle of the Sun." 2012.

Bible

Holy Bible, Authorized or King James Version, Heirloom Bible Publishers, Wichita, Kansas, 1964.

Correspondence

Stump, Danielle. Electronic Correspondence, June 29, 2015.

Endnotes

[1]William L. Montell, *Tales from Kentucky Doctors* (Lexington: The University of Kentucky Press, 2008), 214.

[2]Lucy Mair, *Witchcraft* (New York: McGraw-Hill, 1969), 47-48.

[3]Gerald Gardner, *The Meaning of Witchcraft* (New York: Samuel Weiser Inc., 1971), 9.

[4]George Constabe, *The Neanderthals: The Emergence of Man* (New York: Time-Life Books, 1973; reprint, 1974), 39.

[5]Donald Johanson & Maitland Edey, *Lucy, The Beginnings of Humankind* (New York: Touchstone, 1990), 20.

[6]George Constabe, *The Neanderthals: The Emergence of Man* (New York: Time-Life Books, 1973), 97.

[7]Ibid., 101.

[8]Ibid., 112.

[9]Herbert Wendt, *In Search of Adam* (Boston: Houghton Mifflin Company, 1956), 341.

[10]Ibid., 502.

[11]Jacques Bordaz, *Tools of the Old and New Stone Age* (New York: Natural History Press, 1970), 108.

[12]Jacobs Stern, *General Anthropology* (New York, 1960), 200.

[13]Ibid., 201.

[14]P. V. Glob, *The Bog People Iron Age Man Preserved* (U. S. A. ,1970), 108.

[15]Leslie Spier, "Druids," in *Colliers Encyclopedia*, VIII: 185.

[16]R. Koch, *The Book of Signs* (New York, 1955), 185.

[17]Lucy Mair, *Witchcraft* (New York: McGraw Hill, 1969), 25.

[18]Ronald Seth, *Witches and Their Craft* (U. S. A., 1964), 55.

[19]Ibid., 39.

[20]"Religion," *Life Magazine* (October 1964), 55.

[21]Arthur Weigall, *The Paganism in Our Christianity* (London), 238.

[22]Ibid., 239.

[23]N. J. Berrill, *Man's Emerging Mind* (New York, 1955), 129.

[24]Marty Haugen, *Breaking Bread* (Portland: OCP, 2012), 419-420.

[25]Arthur Weigall, *The Paganism in our Christianity* (London, 1925), 240.

[26]Ronald Seth, *Witches and Their Craft* (U. S. A., 1969), 36.

[27]Ibid., 40.

[28]N. J. Berrill, *Man's Emerging Mind* (New York, 1955), 127.

[29]Jacobus Sprenger and Heinrich Kramer, *Malleus Maleficarum* (London, The Folio Society, 1968, original edition 1486), 11.

[30]Raymond Buckland., *Witchcraft the Religion* (New York, 1966), 8.

[31]*Holy Bible* [KJV] (Wichita: Heirloom Bible Publishers, 1964), 150.

[32]Ibid., 227.

[33]Arthur Weigall, *The Paganism in Our Christianity* (New York: G. P. Putnam's Sons 1928). 270

[34]Ibid., 271.

[35]Ibid., 273.

[36]Lucy Mair, *Witchcraft* (New York: McGraw Hill, 1969), 232.

[37]Raymond Buckland, *Witchcraft Ancient and Modern* (New York: H. C. Publishers, 1970), 42.

[38]Ibid., 43.

[39]Arthur Weigall, *The Paganism in our Christianity* (New York: G. P. Putnam's Sons, 1928). 212.

[40]Ibid., 151-152.

[41]Ibid., 148.

[42]Ibid., 149.

[43]Raymond Buckland, *Witchcraft Ancient and Modern* (H.C. Publishers, New York, NY, 1970), 22.

[44]Robert Graves, *The White Goddess* (Farrar, Straus and Giroux, New York, NY, 1948), 173.

[45]Ibid., 22.

[46]Eliot Wiggenton, *The Foxfire Book* (New York: Anchor Books, Doubleday, 1968), 9-11.

[47]Ibid., 231.

[48]Eliot Wiggenton, *The Foxfre Book* (New York: Anchor Books, Doubleday, 1969), 212-216.

49 Arthur Weigall, *The Paganism in our Christianity* (New York: G.P. Putnam's Sons, 1928), 230.

50 *New Webster's Dictionary* and *Roget's Thesaurus* "Superstition"

51 Gustav Jahoda, *The Psychology of Superstition* (Middlesex, England: Penguin Books Ltd., 1969), 3.

52 Eliot Wiggenton, *The Foxfire Book* (New York: Anchor Books, Doubleday, 1968), 346.

53 Ibid., 362.

54 *Merriam Webster's Collegiate Dictionary*, Tenth Edition, "Thrush."

55 Ibid., 367-368.

56 W. A. Newman Dorland, ed., *American Pocket Medical Dictionary*, 16th Edition, , "Aperient."

57 Ibid., "Decoction."

58 Ibid., "Diuretic."

59 Ibid., "Dropsy."

60 Ibid., "Emetic."

61 Ibid., "Expectorant."

62 Ibid., "Fomentation."

63 Ibid., "Gout."

64 Ibid., "Infusion."

65 Ibid., "Lepra."

66 *Merriam-Webster's Collegiate Dictionary*, Tenth Edition "Macerate."

67 W. A. Newland Dorland, *American Pocket Medical Dictionary*, "Rheumatism."

68 Ibid., "Scurvy."

69 William Joseph Semonite, A. M. and Nicholas Culpepper, *The Semmonite-Culpepper Herbal Remedies* (New York: W. Foulsham & Co. Ltd., 1957), 98.

70 Ibid., 97.

71 Robert Morgan, *Boone, A Biography* (Chapel Hill, NC: Algonquin Books, 2008), 4.

72 Ibid., 6.

73 Ibid., 26.

74 Dick Ruehrwein, *Fort Harrod*, (Cincinatti: Creative Co. Inc., 1989), 7.

75 George L. Ridenour, *Early Times in Meade County, Kentucky* (Louisville: Western Recorder,1929), 9.

76 Ibid., 24.

77 George Huggins, *Memories of Meade County* (Meade County, KY: Meade County Bicentennial Commission, 1992), 139.

[78]Gerald Fischer and Peggy Greenwell, "A Tale of Three Churches" *Meade County Messenger*, Fall 2007.

[79]W. Fred Conway, *Squire, The Incredible Adventures of Daniel Boone's Kid Brother* (New Albany, IN: FBH Publishers, 1994), 65.

[80]Richard C. Adams, *Legends of the Delaware Indians and Picture Writing* (Syracuse: Syracuse University Press, 2000), xvii.

[81]Ibid., 16.

[82]Ibid., 26-27.

[83]Ibid., 45.

[84]Thomas M. N. Lewis and Madeline Kneberg, *Tribes That Slumber* (Knoxville: The University of Tennessee Press, 1958), 174-177.

[85]Compiled from various Google internet sources

[86]*The Spirit World: American Indians* (Alexandria, VA: Time Life Books, 1992), 15-17, 39.

[87]Wilfred T. Neill, *Florida's Seminole Indians* (St. Petersburg, FL: Great Outdoors, 1956), 79-80.

[88]Ibid., 82-83.

[89]James F. Downs, *The Two Worlds Of The Washoe* (New York: Holt, Rhinehart and Winston, Inc.,1966), 55-60.

[90]Frederick Schwatka, *Among The Apache* (Palmer Lake, CO: The Filter Press, 1974), 4-12.

[91]Vincent H. Gaddis, *American Indian Myths and Mysteries* (New York: Signet, 1977), 174-175.

[92]*Witch Trial in Hart County Co.*, Sandi Gorin, (Kentucky-Legends-L Archives, From Papers of Cyrus Edwards as published by his daughter, Frances Gardiner. This book is now published by the South Central Kentucky, Historical Society) 1920 and 2011

[93]Susy Smith, *Prominent American Ghosts* (Nelson, Foster, & Scott Ltd., 1967), The Word Publishing Co., Cleveland and New York, 108.

[94]Ibid., 111.

[95]Ibid., 121-122.

[96]Electronic Correspondence from paranormal investigator and Danielle Stump

[97]Berry Craig, *Kentucky's Mysterious Witchcraft Happening* (Kentucky Explorer, 1986), 60.

[98]Mortgagee from Albert Howell and his wife, Ida Howell, and Homer Howell, unmarried, with The Citizens National Bank, April 3, 1946

[99]Meade Circuit Court, William Leigh Executor of, Plintf. against John Smock and others, Deft. As appears in John Smock's answer to the suit, dated November 26, 1839

[100]Brown Family papers, as transcribed by Shirley Brown, handwritten by JoAnne Willett.

[101]Brown Family Papers, transcribed by Shirley Brown, handwritten by JoAnne Willett.

[102]W. A. Newland Dorman, Sunstroke, *American Pocket Medical Dictionary.*

[103]Sepherial, *The Book of Charms and Talismans* (New York: ARC Books, 1969), 30.

[104]Ibid., 32-33.

[105]Elizabeth Pepper & John Wilcock, *The Witches' Almanac,* Aries 1971-1972, (New York: Grosset & Dunlap, 1971), 82.

[106]*Merriam-Webster's Collegiate Dictionary,* 10th Edition, "Spell."

[107]Ann Grammary, *The Witch's Workbook* (New York: Richmond Hill, May 1973), 94-95.

[108]Ronald Rose, *Living Magic* (New York: Rand McNally & Company, 1956), 89.

[109]Ibid., 167.

[110]Ibid., 166.

[111]Gerald W. Fischer, "The Bryant Family and the Last Indian War In Minnesota," *The Kentucky Explorer,* September 2013, 37.

[112]Arthur H. Lewis, *Hex* (New York: Trident Press, 1969), 90.

[113]Ibid., 91.

[114]Ibid., 27.

[115]Ibid., 29.

[116]Corrine Brown, *Understanding Other Cultures* (Englewood Cliffs, New Jersey: Prentice Hall, 1963), 121.

[117]Arthur Weigall, *The Paganism in our Christianity* (New York: G. P. Putnam's Sons, 1928), 265.

[118]Ibid., 9.

[119]Ibid., 91.

[120]Ibid., 169.

[121]Ibid., 206.

[122]Ibid., 207.

[123]Kay Hamilton, *A Ghost In Our School* (Brandenburg, Kentucky: Bearhead Publishing, 2015), 72.

Acknowledgments

I want to thank the people that have helped put this little-known story together about a Meade County, Kentucky, historical event that cost a young girl her life. The story is important because it may be the only known case in United States history where a suspected or condemned witch suffered and died from being burned alive.

I personally wish to thank my friend and associate Shirley Brown for her research, photographs, suggestions, editing, and proofreading. Thanks to Beverly Furnival for writing the "Ballad of Leah Smock," editing this book, and suggesting wording, without which this book would have been the poorer. Thanks to Danielle Stump for providing information on Marie Laveau and her husband Paris from her research and family stories. I also want to thank Cindy Henning, genealogist and historian of the Meade County Public Library, who relayed some of the stories about Leah that are herein included. Thanks to author Kay Hamilton, who wrote a book *The Ghost in Our School*, and told me it may in fact be the spirit of Leah. I also want to thank musician Leah Medley for allowing me to tell her and Cindy Henning's story about the school play, as well as writing original music for Beverly's ballad. Thanks to Steve Straney, of the Meade County Historical and Archaeological Preservation Society, who contributed anecdotal material, and to all of the officers and members of the Management Operating Committee—Debra Masterson, secretary of the society, and Margaret McCoy, treasurer. Two or more of our meetings were devoted totally or in part to the legend of Leah Smock, from which the idea for this book was in part generated. Thanks to Kay Hamilton, Shirley Brown, Leah Medley, Jason Schmeidt, Mike Sondergeld, his daughter Zoe, and Loretta Young for being extras, and the entire cast and crew who helped shoot a teaser film with producer and director Eddie Franke. On December 14, 2015, MCHAPS held its annual Christmas Party, and the cast and crew from the filming took part. Special thanks to Linda and Shannon Loose, Larry and Peggy Greenwell, Jim Hubler, the band Order #59, and the Meade County Extension Office for their hard work in making the debut and party successful.

I also wish to thank Dr. Edwin Segal, Dr. Joseph E. Grainger, and the late Dr. Fred Hicks of the University Louisville Department of Anthropology. These men were and are my heroes. The management and staff of Acclaim Press are gratefully thanked and appreciated, especially Douglas Sikes, Randy Baumgardner, and Monica Burnett. Lastly, I want to thank my wife Fran for her help and advice in putting together this book in its final form, not to mention for putting up with me for fifty-two years. Thanks, Fran.

About the Author

Gerald Fischer was born in Kentucky in January 1945. He studied history, cultural anthropology, and archaeology at the University of Louisville, acquiring an Associate of Arts in Anthropology in 1977 and a Bachelor of Liberal Studies Degree in Anthropology and History in 1981. In 2002, he graduated with honors from Catherine Spalding University with a Master of Arts in Teaching. He taught school in Florida and at St. Simon and Jude Catholic School in Louisville.

Fischer authored *Guerrilla Warfare in Civil War Kentucky*, co-authored *Meade County, Kentucky History & Families*, writes for the *Meade County Messenger,* the former *Meade County News Standard*, *The Kentucky Explorer Magazine,* and other freelance articles. He has authored numerous articles on pioneer Kentucky, the Civil War, and guerrilla activity in Kentucky. He currently writes a Meade County Area Chamber of Commerce history blog entitled "Fischer's Features."

While doing archaeology and presenting papers at the University of Louisville, Eastern Kentucky University, and Western Kentucky University, he made presentations on historical and archaeological topics to schools, colleges, and historical and archaeological societies. A current member of the Falls of the Ohio Archaeological Society, he was first President of the Meade County Archaeological Society and the Meade County Historical and Archaeological Preservation Society (MCHAPS), first Vice President of the Kentucky Archaeological Association, and Secretary and Activities Director of the Louisville Archaeological Society. He currently serves on the Board of Directors of MCHAPS. Fischer has been interviewed on talk radio shows, television, and in 2013, he was interviewed on the History Channel's *America Unearthed*.

Frances and Gerald Fischer have two daughters, six grandchildren, and six great-grandchildren. They reside in a cabin on their Meade County farm with their two dogs and cat.

Index

Hamilton, Joe Mack 110, 112, 188, 189

Hamilton, Kay 109, 110, 112, 142, 183, 184, 188, 189, 191, 209

Hancock County, Kentucky 136

hang/hanged/hanging 19, 41, 48, 122, 137, 178

Hardin, Ben 127, 128, 129

Hardin County, Kentucky 85

Hart County, Kentucky 117

Harvest Home Festival 35

Haugen, Marty 36

Heagy, Erwin Samuel 168

Heagy, Sallie Jane 168

healer/healers/healing 16, 17, 54, 63, 67, 92, 122, 123, 171

healing arts 25

healing herbal lore 91

Hecate 53

hell 43, 45, 46

Henning, Cindy 140, 209

Henry IV 38

Henry, Tom 178

Hera 53

herbal cures 19

herbalist/herbalists 16, 17, 18, 169, 174

herbal lore 20, 51

herbal remedies 6, 16, 17, 68

herb doctors 51

herbs 122

hereditary witches 20

Hess, Milton 168

Hess, Wilbert 168, 169

hexed 117, 166, 168

hex signs 19, 32

Hicks, Fred 210

Homan 103

Homan, John George 167

homeopathy 20

home remedies 54

Homo erectus 23

Homo sapiens 23

horned devil 31, 43

horns 43, 44, 45, 125

horseshoe/horseshoes 32, 62, 156

Hubbard 126

Hubler, Jim 210

Husbands, Gip 123

I

Ice Age 27

Indiana 127, 128

Indian Joe 91, 92, 116, 123, 132, 133, 135, 136, 138, 145, 150, 172

Indian War 160

Inner Light 84

Inquisition 17, 39, 175

intuition 162

Iraq 24

Ireland 7, 37

Iron Age 28, 29, 30, 31, 48, 81

Isis 45

Isle of Mann 15

Israelites 46

J

Jackson, Andrew 92

James, Gary V. 17

James I 41

Jesus Christ/Christ 32, 34, 45, 46, 47, 49, 50, 65, 118, 133, 182, 183, 184

Jewish 51

Jews 47

Johanson, Donald 23

Judaism 16, 49

Jutland peasants 29

K

Kentuckians 92

Kentucky 6, 7, 17, 36, 51, 76, 82, 83, 85, 87, 91, 93, 116, 124, 126, 127, 128

King Arthur 47

King Charles II 84

Kingdom of God 46, 47

King James 53

Kline, James Alan 199

Koeth, Great-Grandmother 68

N

Neanderthal/Neanderthals 23, 24, 25
necromancer 122
Neolithic 7, 16, 26, 27, 28, 30, 31, 51
Neptune 45
Nevada 113
New Jersey 92, 103, 127
New Mexico 114
New Orleans 121, 122
New Testament 43, 46
New World 41, 53, 84
New York 16, 59, 93
New York City, New York 15, 66
Norman, Marsha Williams 35
Normans 84
Norse tribe 16
North Carolina 17
Northern Europe 27
Novak, Kim 8, 177

O

occult 7, 19, 31, 41, 91, 155
Ohio 19
Old Horned God 31, 45
Old Religion (witchcraft) 31, 32, 33, 37, 38, 45, 48, 49, 84, 91, 151, 181
Old Testament 45, 46
Onion (Allium Cepa) 72
Ordovician Period 85
Osborne, Sarah 40
Osinski, Bill 138
Osirus 45
Ouija boards 178

P

Paducah, Kentucky 123
pagan festivals 32
pagan/pagans/paganism 16, 17, 22, 36, 45
Paleolithic 100
Palmer, General 178
palmist/palmistry 19, 172

Palm Sunday 34
Pan 45, 99
paranormal ghost hunters 185
Paris, Jacques 121
Parris, Elizabeth 40
Parris, Samuel 40
Parsley (Apium Petroselinum) 72
Passover 33, 49
pendulum 171, 172
Pennsylvania 17, 19, 66, 92, 103, 127, 167
Pennsylvania Dutch 32
Penn, William 84
Persephone 53
Peter 182, 183
Pharmacopoeia 167
Philadelphia 166
piercing dolls with pins 26
planting by the signs 6
Pleasant, Fayme Nell 196
poisons 122
Polytheism/polytheistic 27, 28, 38, 44, 51, 81, 153
Pope Gregory 32
Porter, John Sr. 40
possessed 40
predict the weather 17
prehistory 15
Prentice, George 178
Presbyterian 119
Price, Eddie 143
priestess 123
Proctor, John 41
Protestant 35, 83
Purification of the Virgin Mary 34
Puritans 83
Putnam, Anne 40
Putnam, John Sr. 40

Q

Quakers 83, 84

R

rabbit's foot 32, 61, 96, 154, 156
Rankin, A. T. 128

ALSO BY GERALD W. FISHER
AVAILABLE AT ACCLAIM PRESS

Usually when people think about "guerrilla activity" during the Civil War, the border conflicts between Kansas and Missouri come to mind, enhanced by tales of Quantrill's Raiders and Bloody Bill Anderson preying upon innocent townsfolk and civilians. However, guerrilla forces roamed throughout the border states and beyond throughout the entire war, and similar tales can be found in Kentucky, the Virginias, and other areas at a time when loyalties could be found for both North and South.

This is especially true for the "Heartland of Kentucky", roughly defined by the Pennyroyal and Bluegrass regions in the central/west-central areas of the state — an area declared "neutral" to the conflict but important to both sides.

Guerrilla Warfare in Civil War Kentucky explores the real guerrilla fighters of the region, their exploits and their eventual demise, along with some of the infamous "lawmen and soldiers" assigned to bring them to justice.